Living
on the
Edge

This work is dedicated to my wife, who has stood with me and always given me her love and support through monsoons, snowstorms, broken trucks, lost friendships, and hard times.

To her I promise to work toward making the next 23 years easier.

Living
on the
Edge

A Family's Journey to Self-Sufficiency

F.J. Bohan

Paladin Press • Boulder, Colorado

CONTENTS

Introduction • 1

Motivation • 5

Outfitting the Expedition • 9

Tent Living • 13

Buying Our Property • 21

Tent Life on the Ranch • 27

Movie Night at the Ranch • 35

A Word or Two about Outhouses • 37

Building Our Cabin • 41

Cabin Living • 47

Building a Power Grid • 51

Freezers and Water Heaters • 61

Filtering and Storing Water • 63

Tent/Cabin Stoves • 67

GP Medium Tent • 71

CONTENTS

Living Off the Fruits of Your Land • 75

Campfire Cooking • 79

Starting Fires • 83

Oil Lanterns and Lamps • 87

Tritium Compass • 91

The World's Best Coffee • 93

Open Range, Fences, and Dogs • 97

Country Critters • 99

Homeschooling Our Children • 111

Ways to Make Money While Living Off-Grid • 113

Security Concerns • 119

Firearms Training • 127

Tools of the Trade • 133

Mutual Aid Groups and Like-Minded Friends • 137

Conclusions, Recommendations, and Final Thoughts • 143

Resources • 153

INTRODUCTION

My wife and I have been survivalists most of our adult lives; we thought we were "living on the edge" 30 years ago. Back then, it seemed to me that falling over the edge was taking longer than I expected. As I continued to look for signs of the coming collapse in the daily news, it finally dawned on me that the collapse would not happen as a single event in the course of an hour or a day, but rather it would come to each of us in a different and very personal way.

For as much as we may all be survivalists or preppers, we come from diverse backgrounds with differing educational and income levels. We have unique experiences from living in different social communities and geographic areas. Each of us has a different amount of savings and resources, and we each have our own "line in the sand" we will not cross.

By the time the government publicly recognized the recession of the early 1990s, I had already lost my middle-management job due to the slowing of the housing market. Our savings were bleeding away, and I had few prospects that would replace the lost income and allow us to keep our financed cars and home. We could feel the sand in our toes as we approached our line in the sand. For my wife and me, our collapse had arrived.

Losing our home in the Blue Ridge Mountains of Virginia was difficult, but we had already made the choice to walk down the path that we hoped would lead us to self-sufficiency and a more rewarding life. A life that was not dependent on a three-day food supply on the grocery store shelves and that didn't run to a clock set by others. The setback was in figuring out how we could do it without any money. In a sense, our collapse set us free.

The social environment that exists in the United States today is nothing short of slavery or imprisonment, and it looks like it won't be getting better anytime soon. The government schools are just indoctrination centers for our children to accept their lives as slaves to the system. Today's average American parents seem willing to trade their children's futures for their own careers in order to earn enough cash to buy whatever the new toy of the day happens to be. We have become a nation of people defined by the toys we have.

Freedom was lost in the United States when the family unit was successfully diminished by the current modern era. It is no coincidence that when you look at today's culture you can only conclude that it is stagnant. Once the model for societal slavery was perfected, our self-perpetuating government concentrated on maintaining the status quo and has successfully done so for several decades. The original plan for this country did not look anything like the nation we have today. We need to get back to the vision of our Founding Fathers. Freedom starts with each individual taking responsibility for himself and becoming self-sufficient. Being a survivalist is the essence of self-sufficiency.

In writing this book, I have drawn on my family's experiences living in the Blue Ridge Mountains of Virginia, where I first lost my job; to our move to the high desert of Arizona, where we lived for 15 years; through our relocation to southern Appalachia.

While we were in Arizona, we were living near the edge of the South Rim of the Grand Canyon. But many members of our extended families thought that we were living on the edge of common sense. At first, they considered what we were doing so far out of the norm as to be radical, but once they saw how much more freedom we had and the acceleration in the children's development, they all got onboard with our journey.

One of my city friends decided to see what our new life was all about and came west to visit us. The day he arrived our boys were enjoying target practice with new spring-powered pellet rifles I had picked up at a Phoenix gun show (as an aside: ammo can get very expensive with four boys shooting all the time). He must have been thinking about all the restrictions and homeowners' association rules that govern his life when he saw that all four boys had guns and were shooting bottles and targets off the front deck of the house. He turned to me and asked, "You can do that here?" After being assured that we could, my friend spent the rest of the visit shooting with the boys.

We have met many people during our travels, from the national forests and campgrounds to the 66,000-thousand-acre ranch we bought a small piece of. These fellow travelers were from different backgrounds and had unique stories as to how they came to be there with us. However, they all shared one quality that set them apart from people who live on the grid: they were all survivalists.

The path we took to becoming self-sufficient was by no means a straight line. We took many wrong turns along the way, wasting time reinventing the wheel or getting past our preconceived concepts of how things should be. When we left the Blue Ridge Mountains for Arizona, the driving force was a mix of idealistic concepts and a bit of necessity. But after living off-grid in the high desert under drought conditions for 15 years, we gained the practical experience that would be required to thrive virtually anywhere in the lower 48 states. It was this experience that ultimately made it clear to us that we needed to be in an area with more water. This led us to southern Appalachia, where we now happily reside.

Our experiences living off-grid prepared us for what many Americans may soon face. A loss of sustainable income, social upheaval, political change, or even an earth-changing event such as a solar flare or an EMP could indeed be in store for many or all citizens in the coming years. By sharing our experiences, it is my hope that I can help others better understand some of the concerns and issues they too may face in living off-grid. Perhaps they can avoid some of the mistakes we made in order for them to have a better start than my family did.

MOTIVATION

Being a survivalist starts with being self-sufficient. My wife and I had discussed, toyed around with, and daydreamed about being self-sufficient since we first met. We had read every *Foxfire* book and back issue of *Mother Earth News* we could find. Our goal was to plant a garden, raise some animals, build our own home, and be self-employed. But like so many other people, we had allowed life to cloud our vision, and we soon lost the motivation to go for what we wanted. Social, political, and even weather conditions can change a person's outlook quickly, leading to an epiphany of sorts: the realization that your personal, or family's, survival depends on you alone and that the clock is running right now.

The final push my wife and I needed to start down the path to self-sufficiency came from an unexpected source: the good works of the government indoctrination system—aka, the public school system. We had four boys ranging in age from 4 to 12, all of them very bright and totally bored with school. Their boredom led to common disciplinary problems, nothing major but still troubling to my wife and me. So, we turned to the school administration for what we thought would be the hard-line direction both of us had received when we were in school. We were wrong.

At the time, the principal was a candidate for mayor (and shortly thereafter for the state legislature), and he conducted himself like a true politician. He saw the parents primarily as prospective voters and the students as his future electorate. Surmising that school discipline at any level would have an adverse effect on his current and future campaigns, he avoided enforcing discipline at all costs. Like so many other parents, we were totally clueless as to what was really going on in the public schools.

Up to that point, all the other issues we'd encountered in our lives had been insufficient to propel us to pursue our goal of a more self-sufficient lifestyle. It was not until we added this new issue of the absence of school discipline that we were motivated enough to change the way we were living.

The need for a change was finally hammered home to me one evening during a news broadcast. While watching a story about a 13-year-old boy who had been caught robbing a grocery store, I noticed that my oldest son, who was sitting next to me on the couch, was having a difficult time containing his laughter. Now I admit that I am sometimes slow in picking up on jokes, but I have always enjoyed a good laugh and I wanted in on this joke. Not seeing anything funny, I asked my son what was so funny. He replied that the story itself was funny because there was nothing anyone could do to the boy, even though he had been caught red-handed. Because the boy was a minor, my son explained, he could do anything he wanted.

Incredulous, I asked my son where he had gotten such an idea. He replied that his school counselor had told him that, as a minor, he—*my son*—could even rob a bank and no one could touch him, that he could do *anything* he wanted without legal consequences. I was shocked.

After a short discussion with my wife and son, I called the school superintendent to ask why our son was being told this crap, as well as why he was being taken out of class to meet with a counselor in the first place without our knowledge. Since when does a fifth grader have a counselor anyhow, much less one who would tell him that he could get away with robbing a bank?

A slick politician and true obfuscator, the superintendent deftly tried to turn the focus of the conversation from the school's hidden agenda to why we didn't want our child talking to a counselor.

"What is it you are trying to hide?" he wanted to know.

It became clear to us that continuing the conversation would be a complete waste of time. And we knew that remaining in this school system was not in the best interests of our children.

At that time, we had a neighbor who had three girls, all of whom were intelligent, well-mannered, and very different from the other children in the neighborhood. They appeared to have not been corrupted with the common attitudes found in many public school children. When we learned that they were taught at home, this started my wife and me thinking about homeschooling as a possible long-term solution for our children's education.

Our children finished out that school year at their school and enjoyed the summer vacation as we had planned. When the time came to buy supplies for the coming school year, we started getting a sick feeling about sending our children back to public school. We knew that was not the answer, so my wife quit her job and committed to homeschooling our children. We were fortunate that our neighbor let us look at the curriculum she had used for her daughters, and, after seeing how good it was, we ended up buying her used books to supplement the rest of the books we had to acquire.

The empowerment we felt when we took our children out of public schools was truly amazing. It can be summed up in one word: *freedom*. It gave us a taste of the freedom our forefathers had enjoyed. Now our family was free to travel the country, or the world, anytime of the year without having to ask permission from the principal. Imagine visiting our national parks when the hoards and masses are locked up tight in their prison cells (er, public schools). We could even go to the grocery store when there were no people waiting like sheep in line for the slaughter. Wouldn't you like to be able to have your child with you to try on shoes and clothes without waiting in line behind the 12 misbehaving hoodlums ahead of you?

Most important, our boys were learning the school subjects *we* thought were important—math, English, geography, American and world history, science, reading, writing, and religion—not the mindless drivel that the bureaucrats who now have control of our public schools wanted to indoctrinate them with. They actually would have a good chance of avoiding becoming the misguided, mindless, non-thinking zombies that the public schools set loose on the streets every year.

Once we had made the break from the public schools, everything else sort of fell into place. Without the ball and chain that bound us to the local school district, we were free to, as our fifth-grade son's counselor had suggested, do anything we wanted. By breaking this tie and homeschooling the boys, it became clear that we didn't need to be in a high-tax area. Additionally, we were living in a community of private roads and thus not benefiting from the taxes we paid for road improvements. Further, we paid extra for snow removal since the county didn't plow private roads. Now we were paying school taxes to a district that was set on corrupting local youth. The taxes we paid were supporting a system we either disagreed with or got little benefit from. We needed to find an area where lower taxes would give us more money to take care of ourselves. It was time to leave.

My original survival plan had included all the stop-gap safeties you'd expect from someone who had a good job and a bit of sense. But I had just lost my job to the recession, so my family needed a new plan that was not dependent on having a good-paying job or a large bank account. The new plan included converting a school bus (which I had already purchased) into an RV, packing it with all our stuff, and heading west. There I would find work, and my wife would continue homeschooling the boys. As we could, we would buy some unrestricted land, where we would build a cabin and continue our off-grid lifestyle. It was a simple plan, but there was a lot of risk in that gray area called the "unknown." Committed to the new plan, we enthusiastically pushed forward.

OUTFITTING THE EXPEDITION

My family started our journey to self-sufficiency by buying off-grid stuff and selling our on-grid stuff at flea markets. Having no experience living off-grid didn't hamper our efforts at all. We just asked ourselves, "Without electricity, how would we do these things?" Then, we bought accordingly. After a summer of weekend selling and buying, we were pretty well outfitted with oil lamps, military MREs (meals, ready to eat), shotguns, rifles, shovels, rakes, picks, saws, hammers, hand drills, draw knives, grain grinders—all the stuff we thought would help us get started.

Earlier that summer, I had bought a retired school bus with the idea that we could convert it into an RV and tow our Jeep behind it. It was cheap and sturdy, and had low mileage. When I found out how much the conversion was going to cost, we decided that it would function just as well as a truck/moving van as an RV. I gutted all the seats except for the first and the last three rows. This gave the boys plenty of room in the back of the bus and us enough room to carry all our gear in the middle. The bus was a midsize Blue Bird and had a side cargo door, which proved to be very useful.

What we couldn't find at the area flea markets we found at army/navy surplus or secondhand stores. After sorting out all our acquisitions, we found that we had missed one very important item: a tent big enough for all of us to fit into. We did have a small canvas tent, but I was concerned about it holding up to the continued use I expected to give it.

A new surplus shop had just opened nearby, and I was able to find a General Purpose Medium (GP Med) tent with Arctic liner for a few hundred dollars. The military tent came with the canvas and rope lines only, which worked out well since we really didn't have room for all the poles and stakes in our bus. The shopkeeper took the tent out into the parking lot, and we completely unfolded it to check for holes and tears in the canvas before we sealed the deal. I was satisfied with the tent but privately wondered how I was going to get this thing set up. The GP Med is 16 x 32 feet in size.

According to the sewn-in instruction sheet, erecting the tent takes a platoon of stick-figure men and a stick-figure supervisor smoking a stick-figure pipe and barking out orders like, "Tighten that line!" or "Be careful! That's your home you're stepping on." But the directions were pretty straightforward, and I was sure we would be able to make it work. It was also encouraging to see that I was going to have time to smoke my pipe once we found a place to light.

We bought a surplus army cot frame and a winter-rated sleeping bag for each of us. These, along with our regular pillows, made up our night gear. (My wife was always cold in the silk and down bag I bought for her. Don't make the same mistake I did. Go with the fiber-filled cotton bag instead.)

Before packing for our departure, my wife and I gathered our boys and gave each of them a Rubbermaid tote, telling them that they could take anything they wanted as long as it fit inside the container. This worked out well. They got to decide what they would keep and what would have to be sold or traded at the swap meets. Just recently one of my sons told me that he remembered that day more than any other day of our adventure. He still has that tote, having kept it all those years on the ranch and later while away at school. He uses it as a gauge for determining when he has too many possessions, and once a year or so he declutters his life, keeping only what will fit into the tote. There are times I envy his minimalist leanings.

Each of us had to make the tough choices as to what to take and what to get rid of, as there was only so much room on the bus. We

The GP Med tent, which was home to my family for 18 months.

either sold or left behind our TV and all the electrical appliances we owned at the time. There would be no TV for our family for many years. This was a huge benefit in keeping the boys focused on schooling and also later for more important things in their lives. All developed a love for reading that continues today. We did, however, bring nearly all the books we had acquired, which would help us to live contentedly off-grid and become self-sufficient.

TENT LIVING

After meandering across the country, chasing job opportunities and visiting rural areas in search of cheap land, we ended up in the Southwest. At that time, it turned out that there was a lot of cheap land to be had but not many jobs. In late November, we arrived in northern Arizona, where my wife had received a job offer connected to a company she had worked for in the past. That looked like our best bet.

Our first night in Arizona we spent in the bus, camped at a national forest campground just south of Prescott, which we had all to ourselves. There are not a lot of campers in the forest that close to winter. We planned on staying at that site the full 14 days the National Park Service policy allowed, and the next morning we were anxious to set up our tent.

We overcame the first obstacle of having no tent poles by visiting the lumberyard, hand-selecting 2 x 2s that had no knots, and buying 40d nails to carefully drive into the center of the end of each 2 x 2. This provided a set of poles that lasted as long as the tent did. We checked the sewn-in directions for the proper length of the wall poles and hand-cut each of them to the required 5 1/2-foot length. As for the two center poles and ridgepole, we used three 2 x 4s and two 2 x 4 joist hangers with a 40d nail in the top of each of the two center poles.

Back at the campsite, I took out my pipe and lit up a bowl of Captain Black tobacco, ready to supervise the tent raising. Confident and comfortable in our abilities, I soon began barking orders to my four sons. The oldest, being 12 at the time, was as able as his brothers were eager and ready to put up the tent, but it turned out that they were just too small to substitute for a platoon of men. Canvas is heavy. I had to set down my pipe and help out.

The first task was to decide where to put the tent. The campground had concrete picnic tables and benches at each site. Aside from our cots, we didn't have any camp furniture, so it seemed like a good idea to set up the tent over the concrete table. We fumbled around getting the canvas over the table without ripping it and soon had the outer poles set. I slid the center poles and ridgepole under the canvas and crawled underneath to lift the ridge. About three hours later, we had the tent up and were ready to relax. We didn't add the Arctic liner because, truthfully, I didn't know what was involved and needed to lay it out first.

With no stove or liner, the tent was so cold that we slept in the bus the second night as well. It turned out that having a concrete table and benches in your tent during the winter is a really bad idea. The concrete was colder than the winter air, and when you sat on it, it sucked out the last of whatever warmth your body had preserved. In fact, if you just stood near the concrete, you could feel the warmth being leached from your body.

Looking back, that first day was one of the worst ones we endured. My wife was trying to make the best of it by supplying us with hot coffee and cocoa and trying to cook a hot meal over a kerosene stove and an open fire ring. The only firewood we had was green pine limbs that likely had fallen during an ice storm the week before. Between the soot-generating kerosene stove and the green pine firewood, heavy, black powder covered everything. It floated through the air and clung to our clothes, faces, and hair. By the time we had set up the tent, eaten our dinner, and washed the dishes, we looked as bad as any Depression-era family photo I have ever seen. Dust bowl refugees and *Grapes of Wrath*–weary travelers looked far better off than we did.

I realized we needed a tent stove to both heat the tent and cook food, so I headed to town early the next day with our youngest son, leaving my Ruger GP100 .357 with my wife and the three older boys at the camp. In Prescott I picked up a *PennySaver* and found an ad for two M-51 military tent woodstoves in the town of Pine. Locating Pine on the map, my son and I headed that way. We managed to find the right address in Pine, and I bought both stoves.

On the way back with the stoves, an old Indian man was hitchhiking along a lonely, two-lane stretch of high-desert highway. This surprised us because we were in mountain lion country and had seen hardly anyone on the road all day. We stopped and asked the gentleman where he was headed. He told us he was heading to the Prescott Veterans Administration (VA) building. This was on our way back to camp, so we told him we'd give him a ride. After settling into the backseat of the Jeep, he told us that his name was Joe and he was one of the Indian code talkers. We let Joe talk all the way to Prescott, and I'm embarrassed to say that he was either talking in code or I just couldn't understand his Native American accent. When we got near his destination, Joe asked if we'd take him into town instead of dropping him off at the VA, explaining that he had planned on having to walk all the way to the VA and was actually two days early for his appointment. We dropped Joe in town, did a quick grocery stop, and headed back to camp.

By the time we got back to camp, it was dark. The boys had done their best to secure as much dry firewood as they could, but most of it was green. I set up the first stove and started a fire. Soon, the thin metal of the stove was turning cherry red with heat, and the tent was warming up for the first time. We celebrated late into the night with a warm stove, hot food, and tales from Indian Joe. Wanting to give my wife a break from cooking, at the grocery store I had picked up something I thought would be easy for me to cook on top of a woodstove. What we ate that night is still one of the boys' favorite meals: Tijuana wieners (recipe included on page 79).

The next day I scouted for a new site with ample room for the 16 x 32 tent . . . without a concrete table in the way. After some discussion, the boys and I took down the tent and set it up at the new site. This time we installed the Arctic liner and both stoves with their flues. This made life good—*very good*.

We soon learned how to cook everything on an M-51 stove. I did install a flue damper about 18 inches over the stove to better control the runaway rocket effect you get when the draft and fire are perfect. The extra flue damper helped slow down the burn and manage the heat.

Since my wife found gainful employment before I did, this left me with pretty much everything else to do as far as homeschooling and moving the camp every two weeks (at that time, the park service would not allow anyone to stay at any one campground in any one district for more than two weeks at a time). This rule had us packing up and moving camp every 14 days or so.

After we had learned the ropes, so to speak, we realized that the 14-day clock didn't start ticking until the day before a forest ranger showed up at your camp. This way, we could sometimes stay for up to 26 days before relocating.

This worked well for a while, but it was clear that my wife needed a fixed spot from which to commute. On camp-moving days, she would leave from one camp and then have to search for our new campsite based on the general area I thought we might be, which wasn't ideal for her after working all day. Sometimes the site I had hoped for was taken or perhaps the wrong element was camped nearby, and I would have to find an alternative spot. The boys and I got to the point where we could break down the old camp and set up a new one in about five hours total.

You can have some interesting times while living in a tent in a national forest. On our first day camping in a very remote area of the Bradshaw Mountain Wilderness, I set out to make like a bear in the woods. I don't know why, because I never did this, but this time I left my sidearm in the tent. Crossing the campsite clearing, I climbed over some boulders to a path that ran along the rim of a small canyon. As the crow flies, I was only about 100 yards from the camp but in an area totally secluded.

I was in a compromised position when I sensed that I was being watched. Scanning the area, I found that I was indeed being watched by what turned out to be a Mexican timber wolf about 50 yards away but on the other side of the canyon. Feeling relatively safe since the wolf would have to cover a lot of ground before reaching me, I decided to finish my task but perhaps at a quicker-than-normal speed.

As I looked back up toward the wolf, I caught a glimpse of a gray shadow, just a blur really. The wolf had jumped straight down the canyon wall and was halfway across the canyon floor coming right for me when I jerked up, hurriedly pulling up, zipping, and buttoning my pants. I ran along the canyon rim path back to where I had climbed over the boulders and leapt over them. As I did, I could sense the wolf at my heels. My wife and boys were in the tent, so I called out to one of them to get my gun and yelled, "Wolf! Wolf!" Thankfully, my wife heard me and opened the tent door with the shotgun at the ready. I grabbed the shotgun and turned around to see . . . nothing. The wolf, apparently not wanting to come into our camp, had stopped on the other side of the boulders.

When the local ranger arrived at our camp a few days later (thus starting the 14-day clock), I asked him about the wolf. He knew of Old Charlie and assured me that the wolf wouldn't hurt anyone. Yeah, sure—he just wanted to play!

Later, one evening at that same campsite, a fellow camper we had befriended lingered in our camp until very late. He asked me if I would give him a ride back to his camp, which was a strange request for him. It seemed to me that he was afraid to go back to his own campsite. After some coaxing from me, he explained that the previous night he had heard screaming that was so close and so loud that it paralyzed him with fear. I asked if it sounded like a baby screaming or crying. Then I explained that he had most likely heard a bobcat, whose screams do sound like those of an infant, and that I had heard them before.

Unconvinced, he still wanted me to go back with him, so we took the Jeep as far as it could go in the bush and walked in the last half mile to his camp. It was well past dark, and he asked me to stay long enough for him to get a fire started. As he was lighting the fire, sure enough from the brush just 30 yards from his tent, I heard a bobcat scream. It was just as terrifying as I had remembered it and sounded just as he had described. I let a shot off into the brush, and the cat scampered away. As soon as he got his fire going, I headed back to our camp.

As I pulled back into our campsite, a skunk was running along the base of the tent straight for our main door. I remember thinking that my wife, unaware of the skunk just 2 feet away, was about to open the tent door for me. Quickly I hollered out, "Skunk! Skunk!" This stopped her from opening the tent door until after the skunk had rounded the corner and headed off into the woods. A true disaster had been avoided.

One Sunday morning when I stepped outside the tent to get some firewood to start a fire and make a pot of coffee, there was a heavy fog surrounding the campground. Visibility was only about 20 feet or less. Just as I was about to turn and go back inside, I looked up at the ridge of our tent and saw a bald eagle perched at the closest end. My appearance must have frightened the raptor, because it flew off right away.

Another morning, it must have been a Saturday as my wife was trying to sleep in, she was awakened by a roaring sound outside. She turned to me and asked what that noise was. I hadn't heard anything and shrugged it off. A few minutes later, she asked me again what that roar was. So I got up and grabbed my GP100 revolver from where it hung on the center post near the stove and verified that the cylinders were full.

I carefully stepped through the tent door and found that there was an extremely dense fog enveloping the tent. I looked around from the doorway and had turned to go back in when I heard the roar. In the fog, I couldn't get a directional bearing on where it was coming from, just that it was close. Again I heard the roar and looked up over the tent to see the gondola of a hot air balloon blasting its propane furnace as it hovered just 3 feet from the top of our tent. When I stepped inside the tent to tell my wife what she had heard, I don't think she believed me, but she did come outside to see for herself.

Not being a balloon pilot, I was certain the balloon was going to crash through the top of the tent in the morning fog. My concerns were compounded by the fact that the pilot wouldn't talk to me when I called up to him. Apparently, the balloon got trapped in the fog and didn't have enough visibility to move safely. We sat outside and watched the balloon hover above our tent. By the time we had finished our second cup of coffee, the fog had burned off enough for the balloon to go on its way.

You can expect all this and more when you live in a tent in a wilderness camp.

I wanted my wife to be as comfortable as possible while living in the tent and working full time. To make this happen, I struck a deal with the manager of a municipal park to let us stay longer than normal rules would have allowed. This meant we all could have showers daily and my wife would not have to search for us in the forest as frequently, which worked out well for all of us. The boys got their routine down and did their schoolwork early enough to go fishing or exploring in the afternoons. At night I'd fix one of my famous meals, and we would all hit the bunks with the lanterns turned down. For entertainment in the evenings, we would tune in to KFI Radio out of Los Angeles and listen to Mr. KFI and then two episodes of such old-time classics as *The Lone Ranger, Dragnet, The Jack Benny Show, The Green Hornet, Have Gun Will Travel*, and even *The Shadow*.

As the winter turned into spring, the boys and I focused more of our time and energy on finding suitable land for our future home so that we could eventually move out of the tent. As adventurous as tent living was, we were ready to take the next step.

BUYING
OUR PROPERTY

At some location in almost every state, you can usually find suitable property for homesteading that is for sale by owner and can be bought for little or no money down. This was how we bought our ranch since we truly had little or no money. By the time we started looking for land in northern Arizona, we had totally depleted our savings, except for about $500 tucked in the back of my wallet. That money was all we had left.

I did, however, have the whole spring and summer free to look for homesites. We first had to decide what areas we were interested in. My wife wanted tall trees—a tall order in Arizona. I knew that we couldn't afford land in the tall ponderosa pine region of the state and that she'd have to settle for the high chaparral areas where the trees are more like shrubs. By June, I had found a 60-acre lot in the middle of an old family ranch for sale through a real estate agent that offered the option of owner financing. The land had been bought sight unseen by the current owner as a possible retirement spot. Apparently, the couple had done pretty well for themselves and had retired in Hawaii instead, so they were trying to unload the 60 acres in the high desert of Arizona they still had never laid eyes on.

The agent conveyed the terms of financing that were acceptable to the seller, and we met those terms: selling price $16,500, with a 15-percent down payment, $2,475. I took the $500 from my wallet, dusted it off, and put it down as earnest money with our offer, which included the following contingencies:

1. The buyer was to have unlimited access to the lot through closing.
2. Settlement/closing was to be delayed until October 1.
3. The offer was contingent on the buyer being satisfied about the property lines.

We wanted unlimited access so that we could camp on the property as we planned our cabin and walked the property lines. Plus it saved us money. When we made the offer in late June, we were paying $300 a month in campsite rental fees. We needed to save that money for the rest of the down payment and closing costs, which would come due on October 1. By moving our camp onto the property (after we had a signed contract), we were able to save four months of rental fees for the down payment. That $1,200 added to the $500 earnest money left us just $775 short of the 15 percent down payment we contracted for on the $16,500 lot. Fortunately, the closing costs were minimal since, at that time, Arizona allowed closings to be done by the title company instead of by lawyers. Also, we closed late in the year, which kept the prorated taxes lower. All said, the closing costs were estimated to be another $200. I knew that if I couldn't find a part-time job for the last $975 due, I could always sell my Jeep.

The important thing was that we had our land. We would no longer be nomadic tent dwellers. We'd still be tent dwellers until we built our cabin, but we could stay put on our own land. When the time came, after the deal had been struck, we broke camp for the last time. My wife headed off to work, and the boys and I packed up the bus and moved out onto our land. We pitched the tent on some high ground in a grove of tall, old-growth, shag-bark juniper trees.

Again, we felt free. There was no one to check with about where we could set up camp, or no one telling us we had to leave at a certain time. Even our dogs could be let loose on our 60-acre lot without concern. Life was good.

We made it through closing without selling the Jeep, and as soon as the deed was filed at the courthouse, we broke ground on the cabin. It was difficult for me not to get started on the cabin that summer, but I waited until the sale was final. We had to be sure there were no issues that would cancel the deal. If the sale didn't go through, any improvements or buildings we'd started would have gone to the seller.

When we bought the land, we were more concerned with privacy and low taxes than growing seasons and climate zones, although these issues would later become important. If we had paid closer attention to the climate and water supply, we might have been able to stay at our desert ranch forever. As it happened, we only stayed there for about 15 years.

PROPERTY-BUYING TIPS

Many homesteaders and survivalists begin their journeys in far better financial condition than we did. When we arrived in Arizona, we had $500 in savings and a tent we called home. It is much more comfortable to search for land that you can live off when you have a good job and a permanent home. We thought we'd have that luxury when we first started dreaming of becoming self-sufficient, but things don't always work out the way you plan.

Here are some tips to follow for buying property with little or no money when you are ready to start looking for your piece of ground.

*   *Have some money.* I know this sounds contradictory, but you really are not buying with little or no money. You are buying with little or no money all at once. The term *earnest money* refers to the part of the deposit/down payment you give with the offer. It says to the seller, "Hey, I am serious about wanting this property." You *need* to have this. Give up a summer of eating out at your favorite restaurant, and you'll have $500 in no time. Anything less than $500 looks like you are dealing from a weak position; anything more makes you look too eager.

- *Look for listings that have been on the market for a long time.* A seller who has not sold his property after a year or more on the market is more likely to be creative with you than the seller whose property was listed last week.
- *Look for OWC (owner will carry) or OMC (owner may carry) in the listing.* Either way, this means that you will not have to go through a bank. If the seller has done this before, he may not even require a credit check. He will be holding the first deed of trust on the property, and that's all he really needs. If you default, he is first in line to get the property back.
- *Ask for a delayed closing.* The worst thing the seller can say is no, but he may be willing to delay closing past the typical 30–60 days. Any amount of time he delays is more time for you to get the rest of the funds you need to close. Time really is money. Also, use this time to search for the property lines and corners. If you can find the pins at all the corners, you may not want the added expense of a survey.
- *Ask for unlimited access to the property before closing.* This tactic usually works well with raw land, but don't expect it to work with a house or cabin on the property. Unlimited access will allow you to camp out on the property while you save more money for closing.
- *If the property has a cabin or a house on it that is unoccupied, ask the seller to rent it to you for six months and have 80 percent of the rent go toward the down payment.* This tactic has also worked for me when purchasing houses. In the past, I have also negotiated for 100 percent of the rent for six months to be applied toward the down payment. That's like living rent free for six months!
- *Know what you are willing to compromise on but ask for it all.* You never know—you just might get it.
- *Remember the statute of frauds.* Simply put, this legal principle means that anything and everything you think is a part of the deal must be in writing and signed on the offer/contract.

If it isn't in writing, it means nothing. I have had dealings with both honest and dishonest real estate agents. Trust none of them. Even an honest agent can make a mistake that ends up costing you. Have an outline of your offer with all the points of concern written out and double-checked before you make your offer.

- *Review the contract to be sure it covers all these points before you sign it.*

TENT LIFE
ON THE RANCH

Once we moved onto our property, tent life got a whole lot better for all of us. Knowing that we didn't have to move the tent again, we could make the setup more permanent and we were able to unload the bus completely and access some of the hand tools we had brought with us.

One of the first "home improvements" I made to our site was to the "bathroom." I was able to dig a trench at the back corner and set up our solar shower bag and military canvas shower into a more permanent arrangement. Using some spare tarps, I walled off a back corner of the tent, yielding a 6 x 8 area with one of the 10-foot, 6-inch center posts as the inside corner. On that post we mounted a heavy-duty plant hanger, which stood out about a foot from the post. From the hanger we could hang either a solar shower bag or military shower bag.

I should point out that the solar shower bag works great when you have two bags per person and sunny days that last long into the night. Not wanting to schedule our lives around the solar bags, we ended up heating all our water on the woodstoves in a large stockpot. We would then pour the hot water into the military shower bags using a large kettle. For those not familiar with a military shower bag, we found a new surplus canvas shower bucket, which held about 2 gallons of water, with a large daisy showerhead at the bottom. When you turned the shower head, it opened the flow. If you ever see one of these at a surplus store, grab it at any cost. Ours lasted through 20 years of hard use, which is truly a remarkable feat. When the handle finally broke, I had to sew it back together or face the wrath of the wife.

By filling the surplus shower bucket with hot water, we were able to have enough water for all six of us to get a shower. Even after we were living in our cabin, we built a 4 x 8 shower house at the back of the cabin and used it for many years. It had a door at one end, a few hooks and a bench just inside the door, and a hook from the ceiling at the rear from which to hang the shower bag. The floor was 1 x 4 redwood, with gaps that allowed the water to run between the planks and out onto the ground. It wasn't until 12 years after moving onto the ranch that we bought a propane-fueled water heater and plumbed our shower.

Being on our own land and having a permanent tent site also meant we could do a better job of raking the rocks out of the floor area and laying down tarps so we could have less dirt and dust all around. Plus, camp had a more home-like atmosphere. With a few citronella torches, a fire ring, and some outdoor furniture, we had a few comforts that were prohibited in the national forest.

But by far the biggest plus of our new permanent location was the privacy that comes from being surrounded by 60 acres. We set the tent up just short of centerline of the property. No one could see into the lot or see anything of our camp. This meant that we could use the screened sides of the tent instead of the canvas ones. This was great in the evenings when a cool breeze would pass through.

The boys really enjoyed the new freedom the expanse of land afforded them. They spent their free time exploring the 60 acres, finding horned toads, tarantulas, rattlesnakes, elk, antelope, fuzzy red ants, and Indian artifacts. Over the next 15 years, we would all find arrowheads, pottery chards, and grinding stones left behind by the last full-time residents of the land. In a way it made me feel good to know that our homesite had been chosen by Native Americans who settled there long ago. Of course, we may have just chosen to settle on a Native American dump site.

The lot was mostly wooded, and there was plenty of deadwood suitable for burning lying around everywhere. Even after 15 years, we still had not used all the dead wood from the land.

As for the location of the privy, we had several options from which we could choose. All the options contained binding clauses governing the required distance from camp, the burning of toilet paper, and the prompt return of any small shovels or spades taken on necessary trips.

Before too long I met a neighbor with a backhoe, whom I had dig two outhouse pits for us at a very reasonable cost. (I would recommend having two privy pits dug when you have the chance to do so.) Hiring this out was one of the better choices I have ever made. As it turned out, even if we had started to dig our own pit using shovels, we never would have been able to break through a layer of rock discovered just 18 inches below the surface. We then made a very nice 4 x 8 outhouse that could be moved to the other pit location if needed.

We soon learned that one of our neighbors had bought a new gas range (one that readily converted to LP gas) and was ready to sell the old one. Once my wife caught wind of it, I *had* to get the oven. I think it was about $40, but the price didn't matter. It just needed a good cleaning, but I did have to go back out and buy a 100-pound propane tank and have it filled. This all happened before our first Thanksgiving in Arizona. That Thanksgiving was one of the best we ever had. There in the tent, with our recently acquired propane range and two M-51 woodstoves going, my wife cooked a traditional Thanksgiving meal with a 32-pound bird and all the trimmings, and the few neighbors we had all came over for the event. We had a lot to be thankful for!

The area we settled in was a long way from any modern city of any size. Cell phone reception was available only along the interstate highways if at all, and dead zones were all around us. The local town didn't have any stoplights and still had the "you're an outsider if your granddaddy wasn't born here" attitude toward newbies. Few of the local townspeople were ever friendly to us. I later learned that this resentment was because they had been born into this impoverished, remote region and were unable to earn enough to purchase the surrounding land themselves. They assumed we were rich because we could afford to buy the land. I found this to be very funny. Here we were living in a tent and using oil lamps while they lived in town in actual houses, and they resented us because they thought we were rich. That was rich!

This resentment never changed. Even 15 years later when we sold our ranch and went back East, we were still considered newcomers. Our friends who stayed on are still outsiders to this day. Be prepared for a similar situation if you relocate to an insular area.

The folks who settled out where we lived were different though. They were newcomers like us who understood the sacrifices and hardships necessary to live in freedom. Most of them had never seen a GP Med tent except on the TV show *M*A*S*H* or much earlier in their service to our country. They all started out their journeys living in a camper trailer. That first winter, after seeing how we were managing the cold and snow in a tent, most wished they had gone with a tent instead of the trailer.

Living in a camper trailer in the cold is like living in an woodstove. Even in the dryness of Arizona, trailer dwellers have to deal with high humidity and endless condensation that leads to mold and, for some, chronic illness. Trailers are designed to be a mini-condo for use at places with electricity to run air-conditioning units. In my opinion, living in a tent beats the heck out of trailer life when you are off-grid.

Meanwhile, back at the ranch, we were running around in shorts and T-shirts with two woodstoves going all day long. We could also open up an entire wall to a screen mesh for a healthy exchange of air in the tent. One survivalist who moved into the area after us set up a yurt on an elevated deck, which was as comfortable as our tent but more permanent.

Of course, remote off-grid living has a lot of negatives that come along with it. Emergency medical facilities are usually quite a distance away, so you need to be extra careful in everything you do. Before we headed West, I took a free emergency medical technician (EMT) course offered by the local volunteer fire department and became a certified EMT so I could deal with the first-aid and emergency medical issues we incurred. I doctored the dogs, goats, and chickens much more than my family members, as thankfully we did not have any real medical emergencies on our ranch.

Medical emergencies did occur in the area, of course. One winter day an elderly neighbor of ours died of exposure and hypothermia after being trapped by an overturned tractor for 12 hours. Volunteers from the local fire department were slow to respond because of the 11 miles of muddy roads that lay between them and the victim. As we were on scene offering whatever aid we could, a snow squall developed, and the cloud ceiling dropped to about 100 feet. The victim's only hope was to be airlifted to a hospital, so we called for the emergency helicopter from Flagstaff. It could not fly because of a snowstorm there, and the next closest medical helicopter was in Prescott. The Prescott unit responded and was able to find us because of some quick thinking by the closest neighbor of the victim. When he heard the chopper coming in close to the ranch, he fired a flare through the cloud ceiling, and the brave and skillful U.S. Army veteran pilot was able to land with the medical team. Fortunately, the injured man had previously cleared an area next to his cabin as a helicopter landing pad, which was to be a selling-feature of his ranch. By the time the helicopter left with the injured man, Prescott had zero visibility while Flagstaff had cleared up some. All these efforts were for naught, though. Sadly, the neighbor died later that day in the hospital.

Later we bought a GPS that could pinpoint our location for an evacuation helicopter. I recommend that you find out the direct phone number for the nearest medical evacuation helicopter service and have your GPS coordinates written down as well. When a life-threatening accident occurs, you'll be ready to make the call yourself. Of course, you can't count on fire and rescue personnel being able to respond in all weather and road conditions. You need to have some basic medical knowledge and equipment yourself.

Another friend we had met at the Grand Canyon went missing one wintry day. She unexpectedly hadn't shown up for work, and no one had heard from her or knew where to look for her. There had been a heavy snow the day she went missing, and most people thought she had been snowed in. Several days later we learned that she had slid off the road, possibly avoiding an elk, and gone down a steep embankment. She struck a large ponderosa pine at the bottom of the hill, and her vehicle was covered by the snow. She died of her injuries before she was found. She lived alone and kept her private life private. This, combined with living off-grid in a remote area, may have cost our friend her life.

Being self-sufficient means not having many services that city-dwellers take for granted. Of course, soon many city dwellers may not have those services available either. One such service many people take for granted is city water. But not us.

Our ranch was located 11 miles from a paved road and another 10 miles to the closest town, which supplied our water. It did not arrive from a pipe at the end of the driveway. We had to haul it from town. The alternatives were bleak. We could not count on getting enough rain through the summer months, and the cost of drilling a well was prohibitive. So, like nearly everyone in the rural Southwest, we hauled our water from town. (More about this in "Filtering and Storing Water," page 63.)

And, of course, we did not have electric service. Many people think of power as an entitlement, but we were required to sign an acknowledgment while closing on our ranch that we fully understood that the power company had no intention of running electricity to our ranch at anytime in the foreseeable future. Further, we understood that if we wanted electric service to our ranch, we had to pay the entire cost up front. I did a quick mental calculation of $500 per power pole plus the cost of wire for 11 miles and came to the conclusion that I could buy a lot of solar panels with that much money.

Another luxury town and city dwellers take for granted is pizza. Take my word for it, no one is going to deliver pizza 11 miles off-road, and good pizza from the big city doesn't travel 60 miles very well. I often thought I should open a pizza-delivery business out on the ranch. Everyone we knew would have paid top dollar for pizza delivery.

The hunger for good pizza haunted all of us. Then one night while I was making Indian fry bread at home, a lightbulb went off in my head. During our next visit to the big city, I bought mozzarella, pepperoni, and pizza sauce. When I got home, I explained my idea to my wife, who immediately began making Indian fry bread. As soon as each piece came out of the oil, I had the boys top off their own personal pizzas (using the fry bread as pizza crust) the way they wanted and put them in the heated oven. About 15 minutes later, we were eating the best pizza we'd ever had. I challenge all of you to try this pizza at home. You'll never do pizza any other way. (For this and other recipes, see "Campfire Cooking," pages 79–82.)

MOVIE NIGHT
AT THE RANCH

Being off-grid did not stop us from enjoying a movie from time to time, even while living in a tent. Already having a 400-watt, 12-volt power inverter that we bought at a truck stop, we picked up an inexpensive TV-VCR combo at Walmart and a heavy-duty outdoor extension cord at Home Depot. Our once-a-month trips to the big city allowed us to buy the latest movies and, of course, the classics.

Back at the campsite, I parked the truck downwind and about 75 feet away from the tent. Most power inverters at that time came with clamps that went to each terminal of the battery. Today, they come with cigarette lighter plugs, which might be easier. We had to find a spot on top of the engine on which to balance the inverter and still have it stay connected to the battery once we gently laid the hood back down. Of course, we did not close the hood completely, as this would have broken the inverter.

Looking back, I should have permanently mounted the inverter to the truck's inner fender and fed the extension cord up from the bottom of the truck. This would have made everything a lot easier, and it would have allowed us to close the hood completely on rainy days. The cost per hour of this system was more than a gas or diesel generator would have been, but we already owned the truck and could not afford the luxury of a generator.

Once a week on movie night, we all patiently (some rather impatiently) waited until dark. After the stove-top popcorn was ready, someone would blow out the oil lamps in the tent, and then I would send one of the boys to start the truck while I set up the theater equipment. We could watch movies as long as there was gas in the truck. More often than not, this is exactly what we did. As a backup, we kept at least 5 gallons of gas in cans so that we could always make it back into town to get more.

What we learned from movie nights was that we could run nearly any small electrical appliance off an inexpensive power inverter. These inverters are available at most truck stops, Walmarts, Sam's Clubs, and big-box lumberyards all over the country. Compared to what most solar electric suppliers want you to purchase, we could buy as many as 20 inexpensive inverters compared to the one they suggested. Granted, the more expensive model might have powered a toaster or a hair dryer, but we had the stove and a towel to cover those tasks.

Generator, solar panels, and batteries for storage would all come later, but we really enjoyed movie nights at the ranch, especially inside the tent.

A WORD OR TWO
ABOUT OUTHOUSES

For matters of convenience, we actually built the outhouse before we started on the cabin. It was a 4 x 8 wooden, 2 x 4 framed shed with T1-11 wood siding, a custom-made door, and one small window. Having never built an outhouse before, I didn't know to frame a large vent/flue or chimney at the back wall. When I later realized this was needed, I had to go back and add the flue wall.

By positioning the back wall of the outhouse toward the best solar exposure and painting that wall a darker color, the sunlight will heat the wall and create a natural draft or airflow up the chimney and out of the outhouse (see drawing on next page).

None of us spent a lot of time in the outhouse anyhow, and we didn't leave a lot of reading material in there either. We did add water and Rid-X to the pit every six months or so. Arizona is so dry that there was never enough moisture in the pit to aid in keeping the waste down.

Paper buildup was the biggest issue for us. If I build another outhouse, it will be a little bigger and have both the vent and a small stove for burning paper.

The outhouse at our current cabin back East started out as a home-built composting system. I had read several good books on the subject and designed what I thought would be a good system based on all I had learned. Later I found a great deal on an Envirolet composting toilet (www.envirolet.com). It is a complete system already

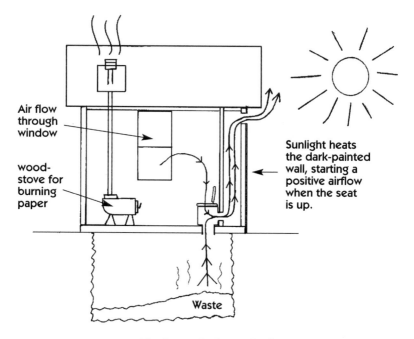

Air flow through window

wood-stove for burning paper

Sunlight heats the dark-painted wall, starting a positive airflow when the seat is up.

Waste

The Better Outhouse Design

designed and approved by the Uniform Building Code. It can be installed inside the cabin just as a normal flush toilet would be. This was better for our eastern cabin due to three factors:

- *Age.* We were not getting any younger and found there were times (especially at night) that we needed to be closer to the privy.
- *Snow.* Our eastern cabin was in an area that has all four seasons. Snow, ice, and darkness are not a good combination for us old folks.
- *Bears.* We wanted to live in harmony with the local bears as much as we possibly could. Going out at night, I have had several unexpected encounters that sent me running to the privy! Staying indoors at night just seemed like a better idea.

The outhouse was placed downwind from our Arizona cabin.

BUILDING
OUR CABIN

After my wife left for work each day, the boys and I dealt with homeschooling, keeping the camp in good order, and building the cabin.

Being open range for the last 100 years, the ranch had cattle trails all over it. One such trail was midway up a hill and ended at a large outcropping of bedrock. After searching the entire 60 acres, we kept coming back to this spot as our first choice. It was nearly in the center of our land, and it had a fantastic view to the west and unbelievable sunsets.

The second option was on a mesa near the edge of our property. A beautiful site, it had spectacular views all around, but the wind never stopped. This would have been an excellent site for a summer cabin and windmill electric generators, but the northern Arizona winters had too much snow and cold for this site to be considered for a year-round residence. Our concerns were later confirmed when another neighbor built in a similar wind zone. They were constantly barraged with wind and dust, and could not enjoy even their screen door because of the wind that ripped through the house. We watched them replace their wind turbine tower three times after being toppled by strong winds.

I drew out a small, simple 12 x 24 footprint and studied how we were going to do the foundation. Having determined that the site we chose was on a rock outcropping, I decided that we would put the

Our Arizona cabin as it was first built.

cabin on piers. We had a chain saw, and there were plenty of stout juniper trees on the property just crying out to be the pole-base of the cabin. I chose the largest trees I could find and cut them at the widest usable base. The boys pulled the shaggy bark off them, and we hauled the poles to our cabin site. Aside from the chain saw, we had no other power tools. Out of necessity rather than design, the boys and I would be building the cabin using only hand tools.

I was able to find a rough-cut saw mill at one end of town, and we used as much of his lumber as we could. For other supplies we ran up to either Flagstaff or Prescott. We built the cabin as our money allowed. At times I would take a break and find some work to get us to the next stage of construction. We regularly scoured the clearance aisles of the big-box lumberyards for rock-bottom prices on doors, windows, and other items we could use. We bought things as we found them at cut-rate prices, not necessarily in the order we

As the boys got bigger and stronger, we were able to use bigger timbers in our additions to the cabin. We had found several draw knives at flea markets over the years, which the boys used to hand-peel these ponderosa logs.

Our cabin at a later stage of construction with a large addition.

would need them. After all, the opportunity was right then and there while we were in front of the bargain bins and had the money.

My wife would come home each night to see what we had completed that day on our home. That first Christmas we were living in a shell of a cabin: no insulation, no power, and an inefficient Franklin fireplace for heat. We did, however, have our Dietz oil lanterns and propane oven, which made life infinitely more bearable.

As you might imagine, both sets of grandparents were concerned about our surviving the "great hardships" they imagined we were enduring. We didn't view our existence that way; rather, we thought of it as sacrificing some modern comforts to get ahead. The grandparents knew what sacrifice was, but many people in today's entitlement society find the concept of sacrifice hard to understand. To ease their concerns at Christmas, we finished off an inside corner of the cabin with drywall, wood trim, and even paint. We then placed a Christmas tree in the corner, and we all posed around it for a photo in our new cabin. From the photo, you'd assume that the entire cabin was finished.

The cabin was never really finished. There was always another project or addition to be started or finished. Over the 15 years we spent on the ranch, we built the cabin, an addition to the cabin that was twice as large as the original 12 x 24 size, several sheds, the outhouse, a shower house, and several large decks, as well as various outbuildings for the animals.

Believe me, living off-grid is a healthy lifestyle since you really never stop working.

CABIN LIVING

In some ways, making the transition from tent to cabin was much harder than I imagined it would be. I had made a deal with my wife that, as soon as the cabin was under roof, we would move in and she could quit her job. She made me live up to that deal the moment the roof was completed. As I was on the roof driving the last few nails into the green 90-pound rolled roofing, she had the boys moving everything we had into the cabin from the tent. This was the first indication she had ever given me that she hated tent living. I can't even begin to tell you what a special wife I have.

I went into town that day and bought an old Franklin fireplace at the secondhand store for $15. It was all I could find, and the nights were just beginning to get cold. I also picked up two used, wood-framed chairs and a picnic table with benches. Now, my wife knew that "under roof" did not mean insulated, so she knew the cabin would be cold. She wanted to be out of the tent badly enough that this did not matter. Therefore, she was delighted to see me show up with the Franklin.

If you haven't seen one, the Franklin fireplace is a freestanding, cast-iron stove that has double cast-iron doors at the front and a wood grate (like a fireplace would have) in the firebox. There are no fire-bricks or seal at the doors or even at the top collar, where there is a built-in flue damper. It is easy getting a fire started since there is so much draft in the open design of the unit. It truly is more of a fireplace than stove. I ended up having to add another damper to the flue pipe just to slow down the draft and the speed at which the wood burned. These things get hot quick and are known to crack under the heat if the original casting is flawed. I knew ours was safe from cracking since it had clearly already cracked before I bought it. We laid down a few large slabs of sandstone on a makeshift 2 x 6 framed hearth that was large enough to store our cast-iron spiders (three-legged skillets) and Dutch ovens on.

I'm not really sure what makes a cabin a cabin and not a small house, but I think it has something to do with having no closets. Houses have closets and storage areas for excess stuff and a materialistic lifestyle. Cabins have shelves anywhere you can find a spot to place one, and they are all filled with only essentials and necessary items, such as books, canned goods, ammunition, oil lamps, binoculars, coffee cans, fishing lures, and matches. The walls of a cabin are not for decorative items but rather serve as storage space for such things as snowshoes, bear traps, guitars, winter coats, rifles, fishing poles, canoes, and paddles.

Of course, the main difference may be that cabins have a dog on the front porch and houses have the dog tied up out back!

Since the Franklin fireplace was not really useful for cooking, we used the propane oven, a propane grill we kept outside on the deck, and a fire ring we built near the cabin. In my book, a survivalist cooks outdoors whenever possible. This notion works well in Arizona pretty much year round, but when we got back East, I had to adopt a new definition that allowed for indoor cooking in the winter.

The original floor plan of the cabin had a single bedroom for the four boys and a sleeping loft for my wife and me. We picked up two sets of steel bunk beds (military surplus) and bought new mattresses at Sam's Club for the boys. The loft was just big enough for a full-sized mattress, and on each side we placed a custom-made bookcase. During the winter, we all read a lot. We found every used bookstore in the surrounding towns, and nearly every time we went to town we'd check for books about topics of interest to us.

The cabin had a distinct advantage over the tent: the roof never collapsed under a heavy snow and did not require us getting up in the middle of the night during a snowstorm to sweep off the snow.

A picnic table served as both a school desk and dinner table. One of several points that I believe made our oldest son stand out over his contemporaries when applying to West Point was that he was home-schooled in a hand-built cabin by oil lamp. I am certain that none of the other candidates could report the same.

The next spring, I stumbled upon a great deal at one of the local lumberyards. In preparation for moving an old building, the lumber-yard sold all the old stock in the racks. Most of the sale items hadn't been seen in years because all the newer stock had been piled in front of the racks. When the racks were finally uncovered, I discovered a stack of milled and planed pine boards that were 14 to 16 inches wide by 16 feet long—all clear pine from a mill that had closed in the 1940s. I struck a killer deal that required me to take all the planks right away. Of course, that's exactly what I wanted to do. These boards went down on the floor of the cabin as the finished floor. While screwing down the planks, we found the original pencil marks and notations left by the sawmill. My wife insisted we clear-coat right over these markings to preserve them.

While driving home from the lumberyard, I passed a scrap yard and caught a glimpse of a woodstove on top of an iron heap. I quickly turned the truck around and went right to the office. A short conversation and $60 later, I had a Timberline double-door, airtight woodstove in excellent condition loaded in the back of the truck. One man's scrap iron stove was our treasure. Once I got home with the find, we discovered that the only thing wrong with the stove was that two of the firebricks were cracked. We quickly replaced the Franklin fireplace with the Timberline woodstove.

After a few hundred or so of these kinds of deals and buying each nail and board, we were able to close in what was to be just the start of our cabin, but it was enough of a start for us to give up tent living and join the ranks of cabin dwellers.

BUILDING A
POWER GRID

Based on what we learned from movie nights, I started to formulate a power system that would be affordable for us. Our evolution got a huge leap forward when one of my friends bought a new generator and gave me his old one. With the gas generator, we could add a bank of batteries and keep them charged with a regular automotive battery charger.

We laid out the system so that the cabin was wired just like a normal house with standard 110 alternating current (AC) wall outlets, 14/3 wire, and the wires in the walls. The cabin was small, but I knew we would be adding on, so I put in three separate circuits I could tap into later. Each of the circuits ended at the same corner of the cabin and ran through the sill plate and under the cabin with several feet of wire to spare. I put grounded extension cord ends on each of the three wires. This made it easy to just plug in the house to the 100-foot, outdoor, heavy-duty extension cords that ran up the hill to a shed we called the power house.

We chose the location of the power house based on several things. First, it was about 90 feet away from the cabin, so we could use standard 100-foot extension cords. Second, the farther away it was from the cabin, the less noise we'd have to put up with when the generator was running. And, lastly, the hillside was the best location for solar exposure, which was important because we planned on adding solar panels as soon as we could afford them.

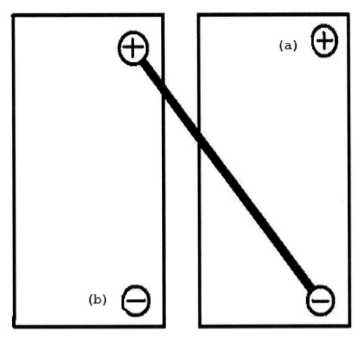

Connecting two 6-volt golf cart batteries makes one large 12-volt battery. Bolt the insulated battery cable from the positive terminal across to the negative terminal.

When feeding power to the battery from the solar panel change control unit (or from a generator), attach the positive lead from the power source to the positive terminal of the battery (a). Then attach the negative lead from the power source to the negative terminal of the battery (b).

Note: Lead acid batteries give off hydrogen gas that, when mixed with air, is highly explosive. Since there exists the possibility of sparks around any electrical system and highly explosive gases could also be present near said sparks, it is strongly recommended that you do not store your batteries in or under your cabin, tent, or RV.

Before we acquired the solar panels, we used a bank of six 6-volt golf cart batteries placed on a wood-frame platform inside the shed. By placing the 6-volt batteries in pairs, they functioned like three

COMBINING THREE LARGE 12-VOLT BATTERIES

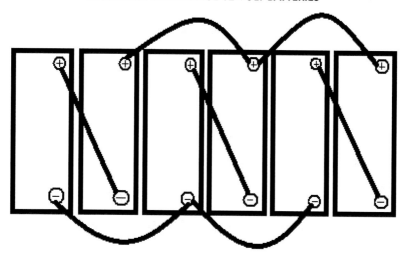

This drawing depicts how to wire six 6-volt golf cart batteries into a super-cell 12-volt battery bank for solar energy storage. Start by connecting the three sets of two 6-volt batteries first, crossing positive to negative. Then add the outside cables connecting the positive terminals. Lastly, add the outside cables connecting the negative terminals.

Always use insulated battery cables, and be sure to tighten each terminal as you go.

The 12-volt power from the solar panel control unit can be attached to any of the posts that are not crossed positive to negative.

All accessories to or from the battery bank should be attached positive (+) to positive (+) and negative (-) to negative (-) to any of the posts not crossed positive to negative.

If you are uncomfortable working with large batteries and direct-current (DC) electricity, don't. Ask a friend or neighbor who has experience in this field for help.

large 12-volt batteries, which were then connected to make one giant 12-volt battery.

I mounted three of the inexpensive power inverters to the inside of the shed wall just over the batteries and used the pinch clamps to connect them to the batteries. Next, I placed the automobile battery charger next to the batteries in the shed and connected the clamps to the batteries. Then I ran the power cord for the battery charger through a hole I drilled in the shed wall to the outside where the gasoline generator was placed. We also built a small shed roof over the generator to protect it from the rain and snow.

ADDING THE SOLAR PANELS

After several years of more important projects, we finally got around to adding solar panels to our power system. There are many ways to go solar, but most options were too expensive for our budget. We wanted the simplest and least expensive system we could get that met our needs.

If you are familiar with direct current (DC) circuits and have worked with batteries, electric cables, and wiring, putting your own solar panel system together shouldn't be too much trouble. If you are uncomfortable working with electricity, find someone who has done this before to do it for you. If you can, barter for the service.

We had already purchased a bank of batteries that would store the power collected, but they were getting a little old so we bought more. We went with a 12-volt system mainly because this was a power unit I was familiar with, having worked on automobile electrical systems. Many electrical engineers will tell you that other voltages are far more efficient. I am sure this is true, but I wanted to continue to use the cheaper, store-bought 12-volt inverters rather than invest big bucks on a suggested system. Sam's Club still had the best price on deep-cycle electric golf cart batteries.

As for the panels and the control unit, we went online to find and order these. We purchased our panels and control unit from Alternative Energy out of Hudson, Massachusetts. There were local solar panel dealers in the area, but they bought from the same place we had found, and they wanted to do the installation as well.

AltE, as it is called now, was the direct importer of the panels we wanted and offered telephone consulting. When I called, the rep listened to what I had as far as batteries and panels and told me what size of charge controller we needed. If you are familiar with direct current (DC) circuits and have worked with batteries, electric cables, and wiring, putting your own solar panel system together shouldn't be too much trouble.

If you are uncomfortable working with electricity, find someone who has done this before to do it for you. If you can, barter for the service.

After integrating the new batteries into the existing system, we determined the best location for the panels. This location will be different for every site. You'll need a compass and Internet access to go online to AltE's site and follow the directions about which compass heading is best for your part of the country. You will then want to

Charger control unit wired between the solar panels and the batteries.

The power house/shed at the Arizona cabin with solar panel array.

This photo shows our eastern cabin setup. I built a small power house rather than use a toolshed to house the components.

This setup looks like a garbled mess, but it works just fine. I mounted the control unit to the wall facing the panels and then set the batteries inside under the control unit. We also kept a battery charger in the power house for charging batteries on cloudy days with the gasoline-powered generator. This photo was taken before we insulated the power house for winter.

observe your site morning, noon, and evening to verify that it gets the most daylight. You need to cut down or trim any trees that might shade the panels and then design your panel stand. I went with a heavy, 16-foot, pressure-treated 4 x 6 post. Since the panels were clearly going to offer some wind resistance, I wanted to have about 4 feet of the post in the ground and at least five bags of concrete surrounding its base.

As we set the post, I turned the 6-inch flat surface as close to the correct compass heading as I could. To confirm that I had calculated the heading correctly, I was able to find a remote railroad crossing near our ranch that used solar panels. I figured that the railroad had paid someone a lot of money to set that up correctly and that its compass heading most likely was accurate.

I then put together the cross ties that would support the panels

Using an 8-inch pressure-treated post and a pressure-treated 2 x 8, I built a stand for the solar panels. The heavy cable was expensive and required tools I didn't have to cut it, so I measured it before buying the cables.

and checked for the proper angle facing the sky. Once the concrete had set, I secured the panels to the post cross ties and started wiring the panels. After the panels were wired, it was just a matter of connecting them to the charge controller, which I mounted on the inside wall of the power house just above the batteries, and connecting the charge controller to the batteries. Done.

I should point out that solar electric engineers probably wouldn't recommend my setup. It is an inexpensive, 12-volt system that uses low-grade inverters. But it easily powered all the lights in the cabin at night (we used only the new florescent light bulbs), along with the TV/VCR/DVD player, radios, and cell phone chargers. Later, it also ran our desktop computer and the Wild Blue satellite uplink, as well as the Direct TV or Dish Network equipment.

It would not have powered a vacuum cleaner, electric refrigerator, hair dryer, toaster, 1/2-inch drill, or other high-wattage small appliance. When we needed to use any of these items, we fired up the generator and ran extension cords directly to the cabin.

FREEZERS AND
WATER HEATERS

Our electric power system evolved into a combination of solar and gasoline generator as a backup source. The two 65-watt solar panels that charged the four 6-volt golf cart batteries worked well as long as the system wasn't drained by use on a cloudy day or a movie marathon by the boys the night before. As it was, the solar power system would run all our lights, TV, satellite, radios, and DVD/VCRs all day and half the night. If the system crashed due to two or more cloudy days in a row, we ran the gas generator until the batteries were recharged. Some winters we would have as many as 12 days without sunshine. During these times we used the gas generator exclusively until the sun came back out.

One of our neighbors with a similar system had bought an energy-saving refrigerator hoping that his solar power would run it. Although the drain was too much for his system to handle, he found that if he ran his gasoline generator for two or three hours a day, it provided enough energy to run the refrigerator long enough to keep everything in it cool. His only regret was that he had bought a refrigerator instead of a chest freezer, since every time he opened the door all the cold ran out the bottom of the door.

Based on his experience, it wasn't long before we made our way back to Sam's and bought the smallest energy-saving chest freezer we could find. I wired a corner of the kitchen and dedicated a new 12/3 extension cord from the house to the generator. We started running the generator for two to three hours a day and set the freezer on its coldest setting. Success! The small freezer performed as well as a medium-sized refrigerator. It never made ice, but it did keep items cool and completely changed the way we bought and stored food.

An added benefit from this discovery was that the generator could also power a small, electric, under-the-counter 2.5-gallon water heater while it was running the reefer. If we waited until after dinner to run the generator, we would also have hot water to wash the dishes.

Having alternative methods to provide your daily needs will actually save you time and money in the long run. We didn't waste any energy we were using. Hot water for our showers was provided by the woodstove in the winter, the water heater (under the kitchen counter), and later by the instant propane water heater. If any system failed or the fuel became scarce or too expensive, we could just move to another source. We now have the same setup in our eastern cabin.

FILTERING AND STORING WATER

When we lived in the Blue Ridge Mountains, before uprooting and heading for Arizona, we had fresh, cool, clean well water right out of the ground from a depth of about 400 feet. Some of the older locals complained that the water had too many minerals, but we enjoyed the fact that with hard water you actually felt like the soap had washed off you after a shower. Drinking hard water was a different matter. We used Brita water filter pitchers for cooking and drinking. This prevented a mineral buildup on our pots and pans. No telling what it was doing to our innards!

Once we got out West, we were slaves to whatever water we could find. As it turned out, we used the tap water from local water treatment plants until we moved to our own land. The tap water tasted bad to us, but it had been a long time since we'd drunk water from a treatment plant, so we were not used to the taste of chlorine, fluoride, toilet paper, and other wonders found in municipal water supplies.

One Brita pitcher was too small to filter enough water for our needs, so we started using two pitchers. But they couldn't keep up with our water use either. At that time, it took a great deal of investigation to discover what today is easily uncovered with the Internet.

After a lot of searching, I found a gravity-drip filter system by AquaRain that filtered 2.5 gallons of water every two hours or so. It was designed to filter lake or river water into clean drinking water, but we never put it to that much of a test. We only fed it relatively clean tap water. The filter worked great and, since the turbidity of the tap water was far less than that of lake or river water, the filters themselves lasted considerably longer and needed far less maintenance. In fact, we are still using that same system today. I have changed the candle filters only once in the past 15 years of daily use, because the candles sanded clean with very little contaminant penetration.

Finding a water filter system today is easy. What has worked best for us in both the tent and the cabins is the countertop model. Many survival stores and several eBay vendors have a variety of countertop drip models from which to choose.

I have tried to teach my sons to always buy the best equipment and gear. Where countertop water filters are concerned, you want one made of stainless steel, not plastic. There are still a lot of choices in just the stainless steel category. Size and number of filters are a matter of personal preference. We found that the largest model with two or three filters adequately met the needs of six people in a cabin. It was even able to keep up with my 36-cup Glacier GSI coffee percolator, though my next countertop filter may be the Crown Berkey.

As for your bug-out bag, my research shows the best filter you can own is the Katadyn Pocket water filter. It is built like a tank and turns river water into pure drinking water just by using the hand-pump design. One of our sons put the Katadyn to the test. He made a bet that he'd drink a glass of water right out of the river. With a large group of interested neighbors observing the outcome, he took a clean glass to the river and filled it with river water, which he then filtered. The Katadyn did its job, and the water in the glass was crystal clear and pure. He made out pretty well on his bet, and all of the spectators bought their own Katadyns after tasting the filtered water.

Water is the reason we ultimately moved back East. Living off-grid in the Southwest often means that you haul your own water. As strange as it may seem in today's world, thousands of people in the United States haul their water for drinking, bathing, cleaning, and feeding animals from town or a central well.

About half the people we met were content to buy their water as they needed it, using 55-gallon barrels or gallon jugs as their transport and storage containers. We too started out that way but soon realized that this was the most inefficient way to both purchase and store water. Like many others before us, we switched to larger tanks to both transport and store the water from the town well.

It is of note that the manager of the municipal water company made it clear that if there was ever a shortage of water, he would cut off sales to those who were not actually living in the city limits. This was an interesting situation, but fortunately for us it never occurred while we lived in Arizona.

We first purchased a 350-gallon tank that fit neatly in the back of our truck bed. I am sure we bought it locally, but they are available at Tractor Supply outlets and farmers' co-ops everywhere.

We next bought a 1,600-gallon tank that we placed behind the cabin and on the hill so that the bottom of the tank was about 2 feet above the level we intended to put our kitchen sink. This point happened to be about halfway between the cabin and the top of the hill, where we could pull up with the truck and let gravity fill the tank from the 350-gallon transfer tank.

It took five trips to town to fill the 1,600-gallon tank, and we never allowed the level to drop below half. Filling the transfer tank in the truck just became a part of our regular going-to-town routine. Even though the tank was dark green, UV-resistant ABS plastic, it was fairly easy to see how much water was in it, or we could gauge the water level by feel. We later bought a 2,500-gallon tank that sat alongside the 1,600-gallon tank.

The preparation for placing the tanks was fairly simple. We hand-raked, cleared, and leveled an area about 10 feet in diameter. Both tanks were about 8 feet in diameter and had an outlet at the bottom that we turned toward the cabin and a fill cap at the top.

Since our region of Arizona did not have many hard freezes during the winter (even though we were at 5,200 feet above sea level), we were comfortable allowing the thermal mass of the tanks to prevent them from freezing. Both tanks were dark, so they heated up as

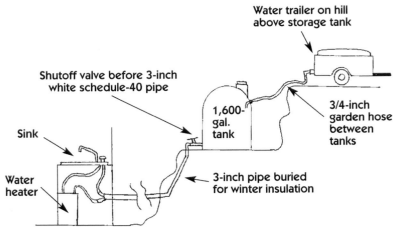

The 3/4-inch tee off 3-inch main pipe supplies cold water to both the sink and the under-the-counter electric water heater.

Gravity-fed water system.

they absorbed the daily sunshine, which helped as well. A friend who lived closer to the edge of the Grand Canyon built a shed around his tank to protect it from the colder climate area he was in (7,600 feet above sea level).

From the 3-inch outlet of the 1,600-gallon tank, we ran a 3-inch Schedule 40 white pipe with a shutoff valve to the cabin wall in-line with the kitchen sink cabinet. Using a hole saw, I drilled through the wall and ran the 3-inch pipe to the inside of the cabinet and reduced the pipe with fittings that ended in two 3/4-inch pipe ends. One of these was attached to the under-the-counter electric water heater, and the other went to the cold-water input for the kitchen faucet.

In this way, we could turn on either the hot or cold side of the faucet, and gravity would force the water through the system with excellent pressure. When we ran the generator for movies or the daily freezer charge, the water heater would already be filled and start heating up the water without us having to do anything. We could then use this hot water to do the dishes in the kitchen sink just like any on-grid kitchen sink.

TENT/CABIN STOVES

Heat is good. It is what makes it worth the effort to get up to make coffee and bacon and eggs. Just keep telling yourself this as you lie in your fleece-lined sleeping bag or under your goose-down comforter, safe in your bunk from the cold, hard world that awaits you once you're no longer able to ignore the fact that the sun is too high in the sky for you to still be in bed. Central heat has made us all fat and lazy, and has cheated us out of life. It serves only the establishment. To truly live life, you need to rationalize getting up each morning. Those of us who have truly lived life to the fullest have been up twice in the night to stoke the fire or brave a trip to the outhouse, dodging owls, possums, and bears.

Getting the woodstoves while living in the tent is what turned a bad situation into a tolerable one. The M-51 stove has proven its worth for many years and under many adverse situations. That said, it wasn't so great to cook on. It burned wood fast and hot, and it was difficult to control the burn. Sure, many soldiers must have made coffee on them at one time or another, but I can't believe anyone cooked regularly on them. They get hot very quickly due to their thin walls and turn cherry red when the fire gets right. I still have scars on my fingers from inadvertently touching the cherry-red stove top while adding wood. Further, the top surface is relatively small compared to most pots and pans and skillets.

When we got the Franklin fireplace, we knew it was for heat only. Not being an airtight stove with gasket seals on the doors, it burned fast and hot, too. The Timberline stove I got from the scrap yard was great to cook on. It was airtight and had gasket seals at the doors and air-flow controls. It also had a large, flat surface that allowed for the use of regular-sized pots and pans.

Our new eastern cabin has a stove similar to the Timberline. We picked it up on clearance at Home Depot even before we bought our land. It was the perfect stove for cooking and heating, and we couldn't let it get away. I loaded it into my truck and left it there for more than six months as we searched for the right property. Once we closed on the land, we found a safe place for the stove while we built the cabin.

I found it after buying the Grover Rocket Stove. The same rocket effect I try to stop by adding an extra flue damper is what makes the Grover Rocket Stove so great for camp cooking. It is designed to

Our Home Comfort wood cookstove.

allow the fire to run away and burn quickly with little fuel. We use it year-round both at home and when on the road.

After much searching, I also picked up a Home Comfort kitchen woodstove. We have baked biscuits in our Dutch oven and in our propane oven, but the Home Comfort stove allows us to use the abundant fuel resource we have to both bake our morning biscuits and heat the kitchen while using what, for all intents and purposes, is a conventional oven.

Our most modern kitchen appliance is the Jenn-Air gas range. It is a countertop, drop-in model that I converted to propane by using a special kit I had to order. We run it off a 100-pound propane tank that sits on the deck just opposite the wall from the range. We use a simple propane gas regulator, which is commonly found on propane outdoor grills, and run the gas line through the cabin wall. It has four burners, and we use it daily. The bottle typically lasts us (now three people in the cabin) for 10 months. We also keep four extra 100-pound bottles filled and in reserve.

The Grover Rocket Stove is great for camp cooking. It is designed to allow the fire to run away and burn quickly with little fuel. We use it year round both at home and when on the road.

We typically cook over the woodstoves in the winter and use the propane in the summer. Having options allows us to easily adapt to fuel shortages and effectively use what fuel we have to its maximum potential.

TENT STOVES

M-51 stoves are still common, easy to find, and affordable. In fact, I have seen these stoves as cheap as what I paid them for back in 1994. They usually come complete with top, bottom, grate, tools, 4-inch flue, and a flue cap.

Anyone considering using a GP Med tent as living quarters will absolutely want both the Arctic liner and two woodstoves for cold-weather use.

GP MEDIUM TENT

I would bet that nearly everyone has seen a GP Medium tent at some point in their lives. They are used extensively by the military, Red Cross, FEMA, forest service, fire departments, search and rescue, and police crews all over the United States. I cannot think of any other tent I have seen anywhere nearly as frequently as the GP Med, especially in the movies. Nearly every war picture or episode of *M*A*S*H* has shown these tents.

For those few who have not seen GP Med, GP Small, or even GP Large tents, they are typical wall tents made of heavy canvas duck cloth (or now in a heavy vinyl), and all have a woodstove flue collar or two installed in the roof. They can be set up anywhere you have an open area of about 20 x 40 feet. The Arctic liner is white, and most will also have screen mesh walls included on all four sides. This is a must for summer use and to keep out insects.

As mentioned earlier, we lived in a canvas GP Med tent as our home for about a year and a half. Before buying the tent, I inspected it carefully and ascertained that all the zippers worked, the canvas had a good feel to it and didn't show any rot, and overall was in good shape without any holes. After a year and a half of continuous use in the Arizona sun, it was still in good shape. The zippers still worked, the canvas felt all right but needed treating, and there were only a few holes in it from stepping on the tent when it had been erected over some ground rocks. It was still a usable tent; it just needed minor repairs.

It is safer to buy a new tent, but it can be expensive, often more than you want or have to spend. You can buy a used tent for much less and recondition it yourself.

RECONDITIONING A CANVAS TENT

So, you either want to extend the life of a canvas tent that you already own or plan to buy a used tent that has seen some service in the field. If your situation is the former, no problem. These directions will work for all canvas tents. If you have yet to buy a canvas tent but you're sure it's for you, choose the best used tent you can find or afford. There's no sense in doing more work than you have to here.

Be sure that the sewn-in directions are still on the tent (next to the doorway). You might need to look at the specs. Also, since you're buying a used tent, ask the dealer for some good scrap canvas to use for patches. Most will have this extra canvas on hand and will throw it in for little or no charge. If not, buy a section of surplus pup tent in the heaviest material you can find. This will work too.

Check the weather forecast. You want two or three sunny days in a row to do what needs to be done to recondition the tent. If you have the wood poles for the tent, go ahead and get it set up in a level clearing. You'll need an area about 24 x 40 to work in. Set up the main green canvas only, not the Arctic liner. If you don't have the poles, you'll have to make them like we did out of 2 x 2s and 40d nails. Ideally, you should use pressure-treated 2 x 2s. You may have to make the two center poles and ridgepole as well. Use 2 x 4s, getting the length dimensions from the sewn-in directions.

Once you have the tent put up, walk around it and tighten the support ropes as you go. Straighten and square the walls until the tent looks right and true with its surroundings. If the tent is dirty, hose it off. You don't want any mud on it when you are repairing and reconditioning it. Allow the tent to dry.

Go inside the tent. It will be dark, but this is good. Let your eyes adjust and start looking around the walls and roof area for pinholes of daylight. As you find holes in the canvas, make notes and map out where they are. Pin holes the size of a sewing needle are OK; they can easily be filled with the sealer you are going to apply to the tent. Pin holes the size of a pencil or bigger need to be patched. Take a Sharpie marker and circle the holes to be fixed. Cut a canvas patch out of the extra canvas material you got when you bought the tent. The number of holes that need patching will determine how much rubber contact cement you need. I had several tents to fix and sell, so I kept a gallon of the stuff around.

If you find an area that is worn thread-thin, where there is little or no nap to the canvas, take a plastic putty knife and gently apply the contact cement to the area, like you would paint. This will rubberize and seal areas where the sealer may not be able to.

From inside the tent, start gluing the patches over the holes with the contact cement. Cut the patches so they will overlap the holes by a half inch for small holes and a full inch for holes more than an inch in size. Paint the area around the hole and past where the patch will cover with the contact cement. Allow this to dry for two minutes and then paint one entire side of the patch and stick it over the hole, glue to glue. Gently press it around the edges to be sure it is sticking to the canvas. Repeat this as necessary to cover all the holes in your tent. Remember, you are working from the inside of the tent only, and you cannot use too much glue. Any excess glue just rubberizes the canvas around the hole.

Now that you have the tent cleaned and patched, you can begin to recondition it with sealer. The first step is to spray each corner zipper with WD-40. Give each a good, heavy spray so that you can easily displace any sealer that may get on the zipper's teeth during that process. There are a number of sealers on the market you can use, but the most commonly known sealer is Thompson's WaterSeal. This is the same stuff you may have used on your deck last spring to seal out UV rays and water.

Use a hand-pump pressure sprayer to apply the sealant. Spray the entire tent, starting at the top and allowing the excess to soak into the canvas and run down the tent. Have a helper hold back any flaps, which enables you to spray all the seams and canvas joints. Allow the tent to dry completely.

When the time comes to take down your tent, look closely at the outside view of your patch jobs. Do they appear smooth and watertight, or are they crooked and have ridges in the canvas that will allow water to get inside? If they look like they need some work, carefully place the inside of the tent patch facing down with the area of the patch centered on a flat board. Paint some contact cement over the outside of the patch and place another patch over the hole. Allow this to dry for 10–15 minutes. Take your leather mallet and gently strike the patch to flatten it out and make full contact with the cement.

Repairs can be done in this same way. I have repaired rips as large as 5 inches in the canvas roof of a tent. It is up to you to decide whether repairing a tent is worth your time and effort. At one point, I actually took a GP Med tent and cut out the center to make a small 16 x 16 tent using the ends.

LIVING OFF THE
FRUITS OF YOUR LAND

Learning how to live off the land is a valuable skill if you want
to become more self-sufficient. Having books to teach you how to
identify the local edible flora is a necessity for the survivalist or prepper. Such books should be a part of everyone's personal survival library. We spent a lot of our time in the winter reading such books,
even though Arizona is not known for its abundance or variety of edible flora and the drought had killed all but the hardiest of those it does
have. All told, we had a few cacti to choose from, a variety of algerita
berries, and the unexpected windfalls of societal living as our off-the-
land flora food supplements. Harvesting and working with these slim
pickings proved to be both a painful and rewarding experience.

Cactus can be cut and boiled, pickled, or made into a syrup or
jelly. It was not easy to work with since it has plenty of needles to
prick you, but it was everywhere on the ranch. The pads could be cut
and eaten year round, but we had to wait for the pears to ripen before
we could make syrup or jelly. The most pain and enjoyment we got
from cactus was in making prickly pear jelly.

The variety of pears we had were small compared to the pears
you see in other areas. I am sure the lack of water had something to
do with it, but even in Phoenix and Las Vegas we had seen prickly
pears the size of golf balls while ours were only the size of a quarter.
The pear had tiny spines that were clustered all over it. Using your
bare hands to pick the pear meant getting the spines all in your

hands. Even with leather gloves, the spines would find their way either through or into the gloves, making the work very unpleasant. We finally started using kitchen tongs to pick the pears off the cactus plants. This also helped keep our hands away from the main body of the cactus, where there were even more needles.

After filling one or more grocery bags with the pears, we then removed the spines from the pears. This is essential because, believe me, you really don't want to get the spines in your mouth. "Despining" is best done by burning the spines off, or at least burning off the pointy ends, by holding the pears in the tongs over an open fire. We did this over the flame of our gas stove.

The despining process is followed by washing the pears and placing them in a pot to boil. We then strained the pears through cheesecloth, and the end result was a red prickly pear juice. At this point, we followed the jelly recipe from *The Joy of Cooking*. My wife's very first attempt was a huge success, and the jelly was fantastic!

After her success with the prickly pears, she decided to try the other fruit on our property: algerita berries. These, too, were painful to harvest. The bush has small leaves with needle-like tips sticking out of them. The berries grow in small, loose bunches deep inside the bush and must be picked by hand. Wearing gloves didn't help at all, since the berries were fragile and crushed easily. Again, we would fill several grocery bags with the berries and wash them in clean water. My wife followed the same recipe as she did for the prickly pear jelly, and the results were truly wonderful.

Each year, we would have to wait to see if the drought was going to rob us of a harvest, but when it did not, we made all the jelly we could from the native plants on our property. One batch of algerita jelly lacked enough pectin to form a good jelly and ended up as syrup instead. Wow! It was better than any pancake syrup I have ever had, so we added hotcakes to the breakfast lineup.

Finding the fruit on our eastern property is much easier. There are blackberries everywhere, as well as blueberries, wild cherries, wild apples, rose hips, and elderberries, all in great abundance.

"ROAD KILL"

The first year we lived on our property in Arizona, an 18-wheeler ran off the freeway and crashed into a small rocky area. The driver survived the wreck, and the next day the insurance representative sold the cargo to a local man, who in turn sold it to everyone else. I just happened to be in town that day and saw the local entrepreneur on a street corner selling flats of California seedless flame grapes for $2 each. Fortunately, I happened to have $20 in my pocket and enough room in the truck for 10 flats of grapes. When I pulled into camp, I told the boys about the grapes and let them help themselves to the treat. When my wife saw them, she sent me back to town for more grapes and a supply of canning jars and lids. I couldn't get any more grapes, but I did find the jars.

Using a recipe from *The Joy of Cooking* and instructions for packing gooseberries in a light syrup, she canned about 250 pounds of grapes using quart jars. We were living in the tent at the time but, fortunately, we already had the propane range. Everyone enjoyed those grapes at dinner time for the next six years.

It was interesting to learn that this windfall of food was not the first time something like that had happened in that area. It turns out that, many years before we moved there, a train had derailed nearby and spilled a boxcar of canned tuna. The locals ate this canned tuna for years.

CAMPFIRE COOKING

Meals on the ranch were always a big production. We all ate meals together, and everyone was always ready to eat, having done some physical work each day. At the height of our self-sufficient food production, we had 18–20 fresh eggs and 2 gallons of fresh goat's milk daily, supplemented by the daily haul from the garden, which included onions, tomatoes, jalapeños, cayenne peppers, and a variety of beans. It didn't matter whether we ate indoors or out, but it was important to know how to cook on top of an open fire, a wood-stove, a gas range (propane), and a gas grill.

Having a good selection of cast-iron skillets, pots, and Dutch ovens is an absolute must for open-fire and wood-stove cooking. They heat more evenly and, being heavier than their aluminum counterparts, are more apt to stay put where you place them. No one wants a pan to be turned over on the fire or the woodstove—*or on you.*

The following are the recipes that convinced the boys that their dad could cook.

Tijuana Wieners

One package of uncooked corn tortillas
Hot dogs (whatever type and brand you like)
Fresh salsa
Cooking oil or shortening

- Get your woodstove really hot.

- Heat some cooking oil in a cast-iron skillet on the top of the stove and toss in a corn tortilla.

- As soon as the tortilla is oiled on one side, turn it over and place a hot dog on it.

- Using two forks, roll up the hotdog in the tortilla and continue to cook until the tortilla is crisp and golden brown. Once the tortilla keeps its rolled shape, you can move it to the edge of the skillet and start another.

- Drain on a paper towel and serve hot with a generous portion of fresh salsa.

- If you don't like hot dogs or want some variety, you can substitute similarly shaped slices of sharp cheddar cheese (Tijuana Cheesers), or chicken, beef, fish, or vegetables.

Note: This is a finger food.

Easy Beef Stew

2 pounds of beef (whatever is on sale: cubed, ground, filet)
One #10 can of Veg-All
One #10 can of diced stewed tomatoes
Canadian steak seasoning
Olive oil

- Cook the beef in a skillet with olive oil and the seasoning. I prefer to cook ground beef well done, cubed beef medium well.

- Dump beef into a large stock pot. Add the can of tomatoes (juice and all). Drain the Veg-All and add only the vegetables to the stock pot. Simmer on woodstove for about 5 hours, or until everyone is ready to eat.

- Serve with a big hunk of bread that is passed around and pulled apart.

Note: This is also a great stew with any meat you grill and toss in: chicken, Italian sausage, shredded pork, or oysters.

Indian Fry Bread Pizza

2 cups flour
2 teaspoons baking powder
1/2 cup powdered milk
1/2 teaspoon salt
Warm water
Favorite pizza toppings (e.g., cheese, pepperoni, peppers, mushrooms, onions)

- Combine all the ingredients and add just enough warm water to form a dough.

- Lightly flour a flat surface for rolling and working the dough. Knead dough until it is smooth and soft, not sticky.

- Cover and let rest for 1 hour.

- Shape into balls and pat to flat circles 8 to 10 inches round.

- Fry flats in hot shortening until lightly brown, turning occasionally.

- Remove from oil and allow it to cool.

- When cool enough to handle, place fry bread flats on cookie sheet and add your favorite pizza toppings (we prefer pepperoni).

- Cook in the oven for 20 minutes or until the toppings are the way you like them.

STARTING FIRES

If you are anything like me, you have been starting fires since you were 5 years old. My dad smoked a pipe, and there were matches lying around the house everywhere. Those records would have been sealed years ago, but suffice it to say, I have a lot of experience lighting fires. Of course, lighting a fire and keeping it going are two different things. Knowing how to start and maintain a fire are skills every survivalist must have.

As a boy growing up in the East, my friends and I used to have strike-anywhere matches. These were great, except after awhile they would absorb the humidity, which was heavy back East, and start to crumble. When they were fresh, we used to flick them so that the match head would strike the pavement or sidewalk and ignite (if you did it right). I remember one time when I learned exactly what "strike anywhere" really meant. I was with some friends, and we decided to play a pickup game of football. I was tackled, and when I fell on the pocket with the strike-anywhere matches in it (I almost always had matches in a pocket—don't ask; I've already told you the records are sealed), the whole bunch of matches ignited and burst into flames in my jeans pocket. That was one time it became very important to know how to *put out* a fire.

Then one day strike-anywhere matches disappeared and could be found no more. They were gone from the kitchen ashtrays and all the store shelves as well. Apparently a truckload of them shared a similar experience as I had during my football match, and some states deemed them too dangerous to allow. Arizona is not one of those states. When I first found them on the shelves of the grocery stores, it was like finding a long-lost friend. We used them for all our fire-starting needs. They were cheap and plentiful, and would last a long time in our cabinets due to the superdry climate.

In Arizona, starting and keeping a fire going was never an issue. The firewood had an unbelievably low water content. In fact, the lumber we would buy in town had higher water content than the living trees on our ranch. Out West, putting fires out was a bigger concern than starting them. We were all very careful to burn only what we intended to burn.

It was when we got back East that starting a fire became an issue again. We brought some of my favorite matches with us, but they soon absorbed the local humidity and became useless. This forced me to do some research. I have tried nearly all the fire starters available, but hands-down the best fire starter I have used is the Aurora Fire Starter 440C with Magnesium by Solo Scientific. In all conditions, this ferrocerium flint steel rod and striker combo throws large sparks as hot as 5,000°F since it has magnesium in its composition. Just one strike into a dry cotton ball gets a fire started every time. Make up your own petroleum-jelly and cotton-ball fire starter helpers, and you'll have a fighting chance at keeping a lighted fire going. We have also used surplus trioxane fuel bars when we could find them cheap. There are other manufacturers of flint-and-steel type fire starters, but I have found that the Aurora is by far the best.

I have also tried a fire piston, which uses a completely different method for starting a flame. It is an amazing tool as well, but it requires some skill in the transition from ember to fire. It uses compression to ignite tinder in a manner used for many years in the jungles of Borneo. Several manufacturers make fire pistons. Just Google "fire piston" and choose the one that best suits your needs.

Whichever method you use to start the flame, keeping the fire going becomes the most important task. When we are at our eastern retreat, I always have a supply of seasoned wood to rely on for cooking and heating. Once the woodstove gets going and is throwing off heat, we stand logs up next to it to burn off any humidity they may have picked up in the cabin. Of course, it wasn't an issue in Arizona with its near-zero humidity year round.

The tinder you use should be the driest material you can find, especially if you have no starting aids. We had been using newspapers as our tinder, but just lately they seem to be too wet with ink and humidity to be functional. Dead tree limbs, branches, and windfall are also good tinder. One winter, we had run out of good tinder due to the sleet and freezing rain that rendered windfall pieces useless. I ended up splitting one of the driest logs I had into 1-inch splints and soaking them in kerosene for a few hours. The result was fantastic. The oil burned off the wood splint and aided in keeping the wet fire lit until it naturally dried out from the heat it generated.

There is a balance to the size and longevity of fires that you will discern as you build fires in your woodstove. All woodstoves start and burn differently. The smaller you split your firewood, the drier it will become, and, therefore, it will burn faster than larger or split logs. Keeping a large supply of various-sized logs is a wise thing, especially in cold weather when you want heat quick.

I know some people who keep a plumber's propane torch on their hearths to help get fires going. I'd say go with whatever works for you, but bottled propane cylinders are not what I want near my woodstove.

If you are going to buy only one fire starter for your bug-out bag or survival retreat, again I recommend the Aurora. It doesn't get wet and will reliably start many fires.

OIL LANTERNS
AND LAMPS

I think **we actually started our journey** to self-sufficiency when we bought our first oil lantern. We were at a flea market looking for items that we'd be using if we were living off-grid. At the time we were fully involved with on-grid living, but we knew that things were going to change and we wanted to be prepared.

Oil lamps have always been a symbol of camp or cabin living to both my wife and me, and as this was where we were headed, as soon as we saw the lamp, we knew that we had to have it.

It was an old Dietz model with a red globe, a small dent in the tank, and a bent handle. I wondered if an old miner had used it as a club to run off a rogue bear, or perhaps a hobo had rolled over in his sleep, pushing the lantern over the edge of the boxcar and sending it tumbling down the tracks. The heavy soot inside the globe hid the fact that someone had removed the wick and that there was a small crack that would cause the globe to shatter when it was finally lit. All this was concealed long enough for me to pay too much for the lantern. Eventually I would buy a new clear globe, replace the wick, bend back the handle, and force this lamp into service as a night guide to the outhouse.

Since that time, my wife and I have purchased many types and kinds of oil lamps and lanterns. Some were also flat-wick Dietz lamps, while others were round-wick lamps, Aladdin lamps, brass lamps, table oil lamps, hanging oil lamps, ships' oil lamps—we've used them all. Just recently we built a new off-grid cabin and had to face the prospect of outfitting it. This time, rather than hit the flea markets, I actually sat down and thought about all the oil lamps we have owned over the years and made a choice based on that experience.

I concluded that the best oil lamp for camp and cabin living is the Dietz #2500 Jupiter Cold Blast Lantern. We have lived both in the Arizona high desert and the eastern Appalachians. Anywhere there was both a summer and a winter, this lamp served us well, and I would recommend it to all.

The Dietz #2500 Jupiter Lantern was first designed for temperature control in greenhouses and, therefore, has a larger oil tank. The larger tank also means that its base is wider than those of other lamps, making it more stable. It will typically burn for 75 hours, as contrasted with smaller lamps that might only burn for 25 hours, and it is actually rated at giving off 1,400 BTUs per hour. Refueling oil lamps can be messy, so a larger tank has always been our preference.

We added a W.T. Kirkman warming plate and a hooded reflector, effectively turning this lamp into our camp/cabin table's centerpiece. The warming plate snaps onto the top of the lantern and is large enough to place a good-sized cup of coffee or chili on top. Furthermore, the hooded reflector directs light to your table so you can see your playing cards better. It also adds to the radiant heating of the room. We sometimes took the hood off on hot summer nights when we were burning citronella oil as well. All said, this lantern has all your bases covered: heat, light, and keeping your coffee hot. It doesn't get much better. These lanterns are available in several colors and even with brass or copper hoods, but we are happy with the plain black lantern and galvanized hood and warming plate.

A word of warning: Use only clean kerosene in your oil lanterns, never gasoline! The first summer we spent in Arizona, I heard a tragic news report on the radio about a young man who had decided to go camping and ended up dead. The sheriff's department surmised that he had bought an oil lantern and then purchased fuel for a gas lantern. The resulting explosion killed him.

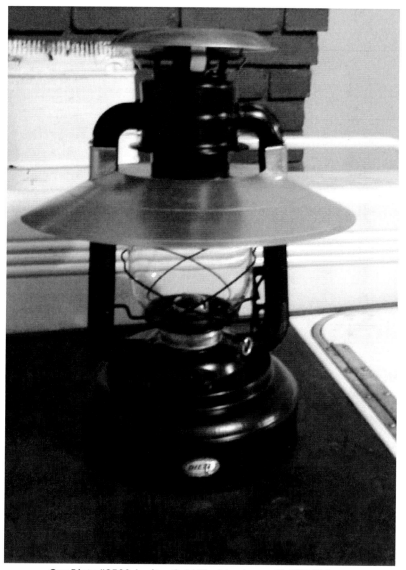

Our Dietz #2500 Jupiter Cold Blast Lantern with W.T. Kirkman warming plate and a hooded reflector.

This cannot be emphasized too strongly: *Be certain you know what fuel goes with which equipment!* As a matter of safety, I ended up getting rid of all white-gas-fueled accessories. Even though I knew which fuel went into each camp accessory, I didn't want my boys to make a mistake while I was away.

One common mistake when using an oil lamp occurs when setting the height of the wick over the burner. If you have ever seen a soot-coated glass chimney or an oil lamp wick that is charred at the last inch, you'll know what *not* to do. This is an oil lamp wick, not a fuse or even a candle wick. A charred wick should be cut with a sharp pair of scissors straight across. Then the corners should be slightly trimmed off. Allow the wick to absorb the oil before you try to light it. Once you light the wick, turn the wick height down slowly until the top of the wick is just below the burner (the topmost metal opening above the fuel tank). Allow the lantern to reach its operating temperature and then adjust the wick height to where it burns the brightest. This is your optimum level. For less light, turn the wick down slightly. Oil lamps should never be left unattended, and the wick height should be checked often. Just like a candle wick, it is slowly consumed by the fire and will need to be adjusted.

Note that some more expensive oil lanterns require add-on accessories to function properly at higher elevations, and these add-ons can be hard to find when you are living off-grid. I spent nearly an entire summer trying to start a pressure oil lantern only to learn much later that they were not expected to perform well at higher elevations (our ranch was up a mile high). We also had a beautiful Aladdin hanging oil lamp with a round wick that never worked right for us until we took it back East. It, too, needed a special chimney and chimney base to work at high altitudes.

TRITIUM COMPASS

One day, I took two of the boys and one of our dogs, Max, to
flag a section line on the big ranch. The plan was to cut a new road to
our property from the east on higher ground in order to help with
avoiding the mud during monsoon season.

The first step was to flag the line in order to know which trees
were to be bulldozed over. I didn't think the project would take too
long, since we only had to walk 2 1/2 miles to the main road and
back again, hanging orange ribbon on the way out. It was a cool au-
tumn day, and we started out just after lunch. Max was as happy as a
dog can be, since he had the three of us out with him on an adventure. The going was easy from our property corner, and we headed
due east (magnetic), just as the compass showed. I'd take a bearing
every now and then, but, all said, things were going fine.

We were somewhere in the second half of our 2 1/2-mile section
line when the skies suddenly darkened. Before we knew it, a front
from the west had totally overtaken the afternoon sun, and we were
in darkness. This would not have been an issue under normal circumstances, but almost immediately after the darkness set in, it began to
sleet. I had seen it before, but I had no idea that a storm like that had
been forecast for that day. It was about 5 P.M., and a very low front of
clouds sweeping the entire horizon had brought a rain and sleet thun-
derstorm to the ranch. To make matters worse, we were lost. Even
though I had my compass, I had not paid top dollar for a tritium

model, and I only had the one that glows for a few moments after being in sunlight all day.

We each tried to read the compass during the lightning flashes but to no avail. One of the boys had a book of paper matches in his pocket. After trying to read by a single match, I resorted to lighting the entire pack at once. We all huddled around the compass to stop the wind, and I lit what was left of the book of matches. Still no luck. I did happen to get a bearing on one of the four compass points and, knowing it was only a one-in-four chance, we started walking.

Nothing looked familiar. We were all cold and wet, so we went to a clearing away from the trees so we could see the compass when the next lightning strike came. When it came, I was able to make out a familiar mountain peak in the distance and soon had a bearing on the road we had been headed for when the hike started.

About that time, my wife and youngest son decided that we were long overdue, so they got into one of the trucks and went looking for us. We met about halfway from home. We were all happy to be safe and to have a ride back. We even put Max into the back of the truck for the ride back (Max had never ridden in the truck before).

The point of all this is that if I had spent the extra bucks on a tritium compass, we would have never been lost in the darkness. Of course, you might say that if I had a flashlight I wouldn't have been lost either, but who would have brought along a flashlight on a daytime project? Not me. At least, not then.

Today I own several tritium compasses and just as many EDC (everyday carry) flashlights. The truth is that I never would have guessed that I could have gotten so lost so near to home.

In the days ahead, I can see a time when traveling at night might be the preferred option for many people and that having a tritium compass (and a backup flashlight) will be a must.

THE WORLD'S
BEST COFFEE

When our walk through life gets difficult, we sometimes grab
for a crutch to make the walking easier. Once you find that the crutch
has helped, it can then be difficult to do without it. Coffee is my crutch.

From the day I discovered it, I have been fine-tuning and refin-
ing the method by which I have been able to stay the course, keep on
track, toe the line, and make it all happen. I have spent years making
coffee on campfires, woodstoves, and gas ranges. While many other
people may also use coffee as a crutch, sadly, they only think they
are drinking good coffee. The truth is that people spend millions of
dollars each year on bad coffee.

Brewing consistently good coffee is an art form unto itself. It
takes years of practice, years of trial and error with many failures and
the occasional success due to some unknown variable. Brewing the
best coffee is a necessary skill for every survivalist to master.

The path to the best coffee is straight and narrow, riddled with
the pitfalls of well-intentioned friends and neighbors who offer their
tepid swill as good coffee to the survivalist. Thankfully, the foul
brew is often accompanied by a slice of pie that allows the survivalist an artful escape from direct comment. The survivalist must remain steadfast in dedicated perseverance until the subtleties of what
makes his effort perfect become clear and success can be replicated
consistently.

Once the survivalist obtains this level of artistry, he can then go on for only so long enjoying the attention and notoriety society reserves for the true master brewer. Soon, the guilt gets to him. He realizes the need for disclosure and for ending the mystery and the suffering of those who would listen to the truth. Let this be my gift to mankind.

HOW TO MAKE THE BEST COFFEE

You'll be drinking more coffee after you learn how to make the best coffee, so invest in a large percolator. I use the 36-cup Glacier stainless steel percolator from GSI Outdoors. Coffee is a must for man's survival, and running out is not an option. There will be times when having leftover coffee ready in the pot will prove far better than having none made at all.

Always start with filtered water. Fill your percolator with filtered water and set on high heat. Take the percolator basket (carriage) out and line with a Melitta wrap coffee filter. Add a quality medium-roast, medium-ground coffee to the filter, not some weak-sister light roast or a cleaning-day-special French roast. Use what has always been the best: medium roast, medium grind. Your favorite flavored coffee is all right, too, as long as it doesn't have the word *French* or *nut* in the name.

Close off the top of the wrap filter and gently set the coffee carriage and basket into the already heating pot. Stay with the pot. Would you set your baby on the stove and wander off? I didn't think so. Creating the best coffee takes the same commitment as being a parent, except the rewards are far greater. The moment you see the first perk in the glass top of your percolator, turn the heat down to low. You can wait until as many as five perks, but you cannot wait any longer than that. Let the coffee come to perk again on the low setting and allow to continue for 15 minutes. During this time, you should be getting your coffee cups ready to hold the exquisite elixir. After 15 minutes, remove the pot from the heat and pour yourself the best coffee ever. You can add whatever you like to your coffee, but you might want to try it stand-alone first.

If, by chance, there is any coffee left in your percolator, remove the carriage and basket and set the pot in a cool area of the counter-top for reheating later. Once it has cooled, the coffee, like any brewed drink, will age and develop a richer flavor. You can pour a single cup and microwave it or reheat the entire pot. Don't be afraid to add more filtered water to the pot to compensate for water lost to evaporation when reheating. Just add a little at a time so that you don't dilute it too much.

Keep in mind that once your friends and neighbors discover the master brewer that you are, it will become difficult to keep any coffee in the pot.

Congratulations! Mastering this skill practically guarantees your survival.

OPEN RANGE, FENCES, AND DOGS

Much of the land available out West is open range. This
means that if you don't want cattle visiting your yard or front porch
at any time of the day or night, you'll need to fence them out. When
we moved onto the ranch, it was my plan to fence the entire 60 acres,
and eventually we did, but it took many years to complete this task.
While fencing is relatively cheap, once you start figuring the rolls of
wire and the posts needed for over a mile and a half, it starts to look
pricey, and you quickly find other projects to throw that money into
(at least I did). We did fence the goat pen, chicken pen, and duck pen
right away to keep the coyotes and skunks out.

Once we had moved onto our 60 acres, I chose to allow our dogs
to run free. This was a new freedom for them, but since they were
outdoor family pets and wanted to be near us, they took to the freedom wisely. At any calm moment, you would find our dogs soaking
up the sun in the yard just outside the tent or cabin. Other times
they'd be chasing cows out of the garden or greeting visitors, both
welcome and unwelcome, as they came onto the property. Given a
choice between a fence and a couple of good dogs, I'll take the dogs.

In dealing with uninvited guests, or felony trespassers as I called
them, I would never call off my dogs. I would quickly inform the per-
petrators that the dogs could not be constrained and would attack if
they did not leave immediately. Usually, the uninvited visitors were
more afraid of my dogs than the sidearm I always carried to greet

callers. When we finally did get the perimeter fenced, it really made little difference in how things went. We still had cows running through the garden after they broke down the fence, and the trespassers still found their way onto our property (despite the posted no-trespassing signs).

I did spend a good deal of time making a heavy gate with heavy gate posts and heavy chains at each driveway entrance. Each gate was then decorated with a variety of no-trespassing signs and several strands of barbed wire running into the woods but ending out of sight. This seemed to deter the honest trespassers. But, by far, the sign that stopped more traffic than all the others put together was one I have since not been able to find. It read, "Cut Wood Get Shot." I am having some made for our new property.

In the end, dogs are essential for security at any homestead. Fences are also required for drawing the line in the sand, and you can never have too many no-trespassing signs.

By far this was the best trespass-deterrent sign we ever posted.

COUNTRY CRITTERS

Having been born in the city and raised in the suburbs, I had little firsthand experience in dealing with country critters. This changed after I moved into the Blue Ridge Mountains (several years before I married and moved with my family to Arizona). The first critter I encountered was an opossum that frequented my back door looking for a handout. My young dogs at the time, Abby and Sandy, understood it was no threat and left it alone, and I enjoyed the novelty of the evening visits through the rest of the summer. It should be noted that opossums will eat anything.

BOBCATS

One fall evening just after I'd moved to the Blue Ridge Mountains, I was sitting in a rocker on my front porch. The night before I had a prowler around the house, and I was sort of staking out the cabin. I had a .22 rifle next to me (my only firearm at the time) and my two 6-month-old retriever-lab pups at my side. As I sat waiting, the dogs found a spot at my feet, lay down, and fell asleep. Soon, I was also snoozing away in the rocking chair.

Suddenly, I was awakened by a blood-curdling scream. I'm not really sure how long I had been asleep, but it had been daylight when I last had my eyes open, and now it was totally dark. My night vision was pretty good, having had my eyes closed just prior to needing to look around in the dark. The dogs were wide-eyed and silent. When they saw that I was awake, they slowly moved closer to me as their nervous looks developed into expressions that seemed to ask, "What do you plan on doing?" I was frozen in my chair. Whatever it was that screamed was only about 10 yards away in the bushes off the porch. My rifle was behind me, just out of reach, leaning against the house.

The next scream came while I was fully awake. This time it started as a high pitch and turned into a low growl. I jumped up from the rocker and turned around to grab the .22, but it wasn't there. Abby and Sandy had the same idea of moving and scrambled behind the rocker, knocking over the rifle. I snatched it up and turned back to the bushes and let two rounds off in the center mass of the bush. Just as I did, I heard rustling in the bushes as a bobcat ran off in the opposite direction. That night, the dogs slept inside the cabin. I checked the bushes in the morning for signs of blood but found none. It seems that bobcats are relatively safe around me.

Later that day, I was down at the community mailboxes getting my mail, and I met one of the area old-timers. We had met before, and I was interested to know what he thought of my encounter. He confirmed that it was indeed a bobcat and went on to tell me about other encounters in the area. Before I left he offered me a warning and some advice. The warning was that bobcats have been known to attack people from high perches in trees. The cat will wait for its prey to walk under the tree and then pounce on the back of the head and shoulder area of the unsuspecting individual, from which position it will try to sever the spinal column, which is its preferred method for killing prey. He then gave me his advice on how to get out of this type of situation. If you find yourself with a bobcat on the back of your neck, you need to reach back with both arms and break his legs. This will stop the attack, he assured me. To this day, I have forgotten neither the sound a bobcat makes nor the sound advice the old-timer gave me.

It should be noted that bobcats rarely attack humans, but they do if they feel threatened or if they are sick. If you do get bit by a bobcat, you should seek medical attention right away, as the cat might be rabid.

My second run-in with a bobcat was the Bradshaw Mountain bobcat and skunk incident I spoke of earlier. And I had yet another encounter with a bobcat. I was walking the ranch with my youngest son one winter day when we came upon a bobcat that was curled up in the top of a dead tree. The cat looked as though it was starving. We felt so bad for it that we walked back to the cabin for a can of tuna to leave for it. When we got back to the dead tree, the cat was gone, but we left the opened can of tuna anyway. Later, we found that the tuna had been eaten.

SKUNKS

Unfortunately, this was not the end of my encounters with country critters. While we lived on the Arizona ranch, our dogs were sprayed by skunks several times. It is so sad to have your family friend come to you smelling so bad that you don't want to be anywhere near it. The only thing you can do is wash, wash, wash. On one occasion, we did have a half gallon of V-8 juice (who drinks tomato juice?) that we thought would be as effective as the commonly known tomato juice bath. It seemed to have worked.

PORCUPINES

The only thing worse than having your dogs tangle with a skunk is having them end up on the losing end of a scuffle with a porcupine. This is where the rubber meets the road. Being a self-sufficient survivalist will often mean that you are the one taking care of emergencies for both your family and your animals. Of course, where life or limb is concerned, you should still take the victim to a hospital or veterinary clinic if possible, but as remote as you may be, you are still the first (and perhaps only) responder.

Max had been abandoned by a failed homesteader, who left him and several other dogs locked in a chain-link cage. After someone noticed that the dogs were starving to death, they let them loose to fend for themselves. Max showed up at our ranch about two weeks later, as I was later told. At the time, we already had two dogs and didn't need another, but the sight of the starving beast was too much for us to turn him away. He was very cautious of us for some time. As he gained his weight and strength back, he filled out to be a pretty big dog. I think he was a black lab and mastiff mix, and most folks coming to visit were very concerned when they saw Max. This worked out well for us, especially when it was unwanted guests whom Max greeted.

The first month he was with us he chased and caught, at least for a moment, a porcupine. When he returned home from the encounter, with about 60 quills buried in his snout and head, I was not there. My wife and oldest son had Max lie down on our front porch, trying to keep him calm while waiting for me. When I arrived home, it became clear that I was the only one who could have approached him without being bitten.

I took a pair of needle-nose pliers and, as gently as I could, grabbed the exposed end of each of the quills, one at a time, and pulled them from his snout. This took far more effort and time than I imagined it would. Max cried out each time, and we all had to comfort him again and again after every one or two pulls. We were amazed at the length of the quills. They had worked themselves deep into Max's nose, leaving only about a 1/4 inch exposed. When I pulled them out, I found that some were 3 to 4 inches long. When we finished the job, he made it clear to us that he was now our dog with the thanks and affection he showed.

Over the years, I pulled quills from four of our dogs, one dog twice.

RACCOONS AND BEARS

Curiously, we didn't have any raccoon or bear interactions while out West. It wasn't until we returned East and started to build our mountain cabin that we encountered them.

The site we chose for our eastern cabin was within 50 yards of a

This is my lovely wife's hand as a gauge to show how big the bear print was.

river, and we were camping in a travel trailer another 200 yards from there. Without fail, any night that we accidentally left the day's garbage out, we would get a midnight visit from a group of raccoons that lived down on the river. They would empty the bag and leave bite marks on everything they tasted. Sometimes they would even leave tracks.

During the day, we let the dogs have the run of the property. They would go exploring from time to time, but for the most part they stayed near the cabin or garden where we were working. When we would go the mountain to pick berries, they all would come along on the grand adventure. Several times while out berry picking on the mountain, Maggie (our retriever-mutt mix) would bristle and stare into the woods. I suspected a bear, but we had yet to meet the critter.

Then one morning when we stepped out of the camper, we saw

that the trash that we had asked our son to put in the back of the truck was thrown all over the area. My wife and son decided that raccoons had been the culprits and discussed how they might live-trap the critters and relocate them. I looked at both of them and asked if they really thought raccoons could do that much damage. I suggested that it was a bear. They both laughed and said, "A bear? Here?" They had both witnessed me crying wolf and skunk and insisted that I was now crying bear.

The next night, after a long day swinging a hammer and hauling lumber, someone left the trash unsecured again. The next morning the same story played out, only this time I had some evidence to back up my theory. The bear had been nice enough to leave a mud print by the trailer's kitchen window, along with a nose print on the glass. We also found a hind-leg footprint in the mud by the trailer.

It turns out that dogs are not the only animals that enjoy dog food. Not having built a feed shed for the animals yet, I had put the open bag of dog food in a Rubbermaid trash can with a heavy lid that snapped closed. The trash can did a nice job of keeping the raccoons out of the dog food, but it just served as a plastic piñata for the bear. It didn't take much for him to break open the can. One good whack on the side of the can and the lid flew off. The bear then had about 50 pounds of treats to enjoy.

A locking shed that is strong enough to withstand a hungry, curious bear is a must when living in bear country.

GOATS, CHICKENS, AND DUCKS

After my wife quit her job, she started what was to be the most successful project in self-sufficiency we have ever done: raising livestock for food. Our menagerie included goats, chickens, and ducks.

Goats

Looking through the local *Thrifty Nickel* paper, she found a goat for sale. The goat was older and had had several kids before she became ours. It seems that most people are not very good with goats, and goats can sense this. Penny, as she was named for her copper color, had been through several families, all of whom claimed she was a mean goat. But we liked the looks of her and she took to us right away, so we took her home. We built a fenced pen area and a lean-to shelter for Penny and started looking for more goats. Goats are social animals and need company. After finding three more does (females), we had a long discussion about getting our own billy (male) goat.

Billies are unlike other goats. They smell, and I don't mean just an unpleasant smell. I am talking about a smell so bad that if your coat picked up the smell from being near the billy, you'd burn it on the spot. I am talking about high-octane stink. However, if you want milk from your goats, you need a billy around.

We found a male whose family lines proved to throw mostly triplets. This is good as far as goats go. What we didn't expect was that our new billy, Meshach, was the most loving and attention-seeking goat in the herd. Given the chance, he would have followed us everywhere and constantly rubbed his head against us, in a loving way, of course. But he smelled so bad that no one would let him within 10 feet of them. It was left to me to be his only friend.

Meshach, one of a set of triplets himself, was kept downwind of both the house and the other animal pens. At first we put his pen between the cabin and the chickens, but the chickens complained too much. Whenever the time was right, we would bring one of the girls to his pen for a stay of about a week or so. This activity didn't last much of the year as we only kept three does in the milking cycle each year. Meshach, however, wanted friendship year round.

Every day I would carry fresh water down to him in a 5-gallon pail. He would meet me at the fence and start calling for attention. He then would skillfully aim his urine stream to hit his beard, creating a heavy froth which he would lap up just as skillfully with his tongue. This was Meshach at his best. At his worst, he would see you coming down the path and skillfully hit you with his urine stream

The pen where we kept Meshach was downwind of everything!

from up to 40 feet away. We did have some good contact though. Once he realized I was to be his only friend for most of the year, I eventually was able to approach him without being sprayed. He liked to have his beard tugged. Of course, I wore gloves.

After the initial startup period of acquiring the animals and learning the processes of milking goats, we averaged about two gallons of goat milk each day. We drank the milk and made cheese from it. We enjoyed this level of production for many years. The only slowdown occurred in the winter, when my wife thought it was too cold to be out milking the goats. This was fine by the goats, too, so she let them dry up and take a break through the coldest months.

Chickens

Much has been written about keeping chickens, most of which has been read by my wife. For reasons known only to her, we ended up with several varieties. They included Rhode Island Reds (good layers and good with kids), Black Australorp (handsome), Araucanas (good layers and funny to watch), Buff Orpingtons (good-looking), and White Leghorns (supposedly good layers).

The biggest error when choosing chickens came when my wife thought that picking more active chicks over docile ones would ensure their survival. The assumption was that they were stronger and healthier. It turned out that she had successfully picked all roosters from the co-op's brooder. Fortunately, this occurred only once, and we ended up with only one batch of roosters. The real lesson here is to order your chickens from a breeder after researching which breeds fit your needs, rather than the "which is the cutest chicken" method while at your local co-op.

Since we knew from the start that coyotes were going to be a threat to our chickens, I built what turned out to be a good chicken house. We did not lose any chickens to predators; however, we did once lose a few eggs to a 5-foot-long black snake. At our peak of production, we typically harvested 18 eggs a day.

Ducks

After hand-digging a small pond, I decided that I'd like to have some ducks. Having always liked ducks, I thought they'd be a nice addition to the chickens and goats we already had. I built a pen near the dam area of the pond, and my wife found some Rouens, which are a type of flightless mallard. We agreed that having the flightless ducks would help them in acclimating to their new pond better and keep them around since they couldn't fly off. We were able to score a dozen adult ducks for free from someone who was moving out of the area. After an afternoon duck roundup, we headed home with our ducks.

The ducks loved the ranch and especially the small pond full of rainwater from the recent monsoons. It was a bigger pond than they were used to at their old home. We enjoyed about a year of duck eggs, ducklings, and the evening chatter of ducks quacking. Then it happened. Late one night there was a commotion at the duck pen. It had everyone upset—the goats, the dogs, the chickens, the ducks, and all four boys were all running around in the dark yelling. When we finally were able to get a flashlight that worked to the scene, we found one of our ducks was missing its head. The head, neck and all, had been plucked right off its body by an owl. There was little we could do. One by one, each night we lost another duck. In less than two weeks, it was over.

I deeply regretted having let down my ducks. I should have built a pen that was fully enclosed, where they could escape certain death. I soon redesigned the pen area and built a new pen that would protect the fowl from predators.

Later that week, I came upon two great horned owls perched in twin dead trees on our ranch. They were beautiful birds, each more than 2 feet tall. They feared nothing and even waited for me to bring my wife back for a look.

We found another duck owner who was willing to give away 20 ducks to anyone who could round them up. Having punched and rounded up duckies before, we were able to take them all. Again, we were told that these ducks were flightless Rouens. These ducks

My flightless ducks.

didn't look as healthy as the last flock we got. They were in a very small area and had little room to run. As for water, they only had a kiddy pool filled with a mucky mess. When we got them home, they also loved the pond.

After about two weeks our ducks were looking better and stronger. One afternoon, I was checking on the ducks and noticed they were up to something. They were all lining up and attempting to fly out of the pen. I went back to the cabin to get my wife, and as we both came out of the cabin, we got to see all of our "flightless" ducks fly over the cabin, circle their pen once, and then disappear into the southwestern horizon. We never saw them again.

I was done with ducks.

HOMESCHOOLING
OUR CHILDREN

My wife and I made the commitment to homeschool our children long before my job was lost to the failing housing market and before we uprooted and moved West. We sincerely believed that homeschooling was the only real option that offered any chance at a successful future for our children. The elementary school we took them out of suffered a loss of 25 percent of the students that same year we made our decision. Our kids had been out of that school for a few months when we received a call from the school secretary asking why they weren't enrolled there. She went on to explain the effects of a huge loss of funds that the school district had to absorb after several families had withdrawn their children from the school and started to homeschool them.

After we settled out West, we did have some involvement with the local school system. Our oldest son wanted to play basketball, and the State of Arizona, knowing that we paid taxes that supported the school, had no issues with this. Later, two of our younger boys wanted to run cross-country track for the local high school, and this also was welcomed by the school district.

The curriculum we chose for homeschooling our boys was from a company out of Pensacola, Florida, named A Beka Book. We can't say enough about the quality of the entire curriculum. A Beka served my sons well from K through 12. Our experience with homeschooling worked out even better than we had hoped. It is one thing to say so, but the proof was in the boys' performance. When the boys tested out on both the SAT and the ACT college entrance exams, all four scored in the top 5 percent in the nation. In fact, on the SAT, they all scored in the top 2 percent. All four earned scholarships to the colleges they wanted. They are now all college graduates and are hardworking, successful members of society.

Along with the A Beka curriculum, we changed the way we ran our household that I think enhanced their learning. The television was used only for movie nights. As for other entertainment, it was outdoor activities and reading. This was a difficult pill for the children to swallow at first, but they soon discovered that they all loved to read.

Each child went at his own pace, completing each course at different times. We held school five days a week year round. Classes began after breakfast and the chores were finished and lasted until lunch. After lunch, it was the boys' time for reading, exploring, and playing.

This may seem like a short day to you, but try doing a time study on your child's day at school. I think you will find that once you account for all the distractions and administrative issues that occur, students get less than an hour or two of true learning time each day. We were able to offer our children a solid three hours a day of book-learning.

Of course, homeschooling isn't for everyone. It takes a lot of time and a true commitment from everyone involved, but in the end, the payoff can be big. Since our boys all earned college scholarships, this saved us (and them) a chunk of money.

If you are considering homeschooling your child, I salute you. They will be far better off for your decision.

WAYS TO MAKE MONEY WHILE LIVING OFF-GRID

A friend of mine from out West summed it up best when he said, "Do you want to know how to have a little money in northern Arizona? Come here with a lot of money—soon, you'll have a little!" This sentiment holds true for most rural areas.

Once the cabin was under a roof, my wife executed her side of our agreement. She quit her job and regained her focus on homeschooling the boys, gardening, and raising chickens and goats. This left me with the tasks of completing the cabin and finding ways to earn money in Small Town, Arizona.

My work history reads like a list of construction industry jobs. I started in high school hauling materials on construction sites during the summer break, and since then I have done everything from framing houses and running electrical wire to selling nearly all types of building materials. I have never been afraid to tackle any new job. As long as the dollars made sense, I was ready to try.

The real question became, "What would the small towns have to offer?"

Among other things, here is a partial list of the jobs I had while raising our family in Arizona and the short reason each job ended. Some of these jobs I never imagined I'd be doing.

- *Heavy equipment operator in the quarries.* I ran graders and hoes from early in the morning until the midday siesta, when work stopped until the day cooled off in the late afternoon. I left this job over safety concerns. The equipment was old and broken down and not serviced well. One day the brakes gave out on a loader that was used in close proximity to the workers on the ground. The quarry owner informed me that the brakes were not going to be fixed. That was enough for me. This type of slipshod operation is common in rural areas. OSHA spends far more time in the big city than rural areas, which is fine by me. But, then again, I keep my personal equipment in good order.

When I first started, I heard the tale of one quarry driver who ran his trucks until they would split in two from stress cracks. On one occasion he was overloaded and in low gear coming down a steep grade alongside a mountain with a Mexican worker in the front seat with him. On the driver's side was a steep hill going down the side of the mountain, while on the passenger's side was a wall of rock straight up. The road was so narrow that, if the worker needed to get out of the cab, the rock wall would have prevented him from opening his door wide. When they were about halfway down the grade, the driver must have been thinking about how his brakes hadn't been working properly lately, and the fear of what could happen must have been more than he could bear. The passenger was watching the road ahead when he turned and noticed that the driver was gone and the driver's door was open. The driver had jumped out of the truck. Not having the opportunity to ask why, the Mexican worker bailed out of the truck as well. The two suffered minor cuts and scrapes from their slow-speed jump, and the truck made it down the straight and narrow-grade road before coming to a stop at the road's end at some large boulders.

• *Owner/operator of a company hauling flagstone out of the quarries.* This job was great. I made good money and worked the hours I wanted to work: hauling during the early morning when it was cool and spending time on the ranch during the hot afternoon. That job ended when the Immigration and Naturalization Service bus showed up and hauled off all the illegal aliens who worked in the quarry. This shut down quarry operations until these illegals (or others) could recross the border and make their way back north to our area. All the quarry owners knew about this yearly event and planned for the lull. Being new to the business, I hadn't. This meant that there was really no stability in the quarries. I had to work, and since it was only the illegal Mexicans digging the rock, quarry work wasn't consistent enough for my needs.

- *Newspaper distributor for the Grand Canyon.* This is one of the most coveted jobs in the rural West. It is an all-cash business and takes just a few hours each day in the early morning. I drove 200 miles a day starting at 1:00 in the morning. Every day I got to see the sun rise at the south rim of the Grand Canyon for five years. My wife and boys often rode along when they could, and it was always an adventure making the 200-mile round trip in the middle of the night. Nearly every night we would see elk and antelope along the route, and some nights we would come up on other people's mishaps. There was never a dull moment. The downside was that I worked seven days a week in all weather conditions. After five years, I was burned out and quit.

- *Radio advertising sales manager.* This job is not for everyone, but I had been in sales for many years and was ready for the challenge. Sales jobs in radio advertising are always available everywhere. If you can sell air, the job will pay well, but you must insist on cash from the radio station. If you don't, it will want to pay you in traded items from the other salesmen's efforts.

- *Cowboy cookout manager.* This was another fun job that actually earned some money in tips. It was a seasonal summer job, which can be both good and bad depending on your situation. I also got to get shot in the daily shootout shows.

- *General store manager/owner.* Ultimately we bought a property in town and opened up shop. We did well, but after all was said, it still was just a small-town store. When we decided to move back East, we closed the store and sold the property.

- *Internet sales.* This type of job might be the best all-around employment for people in rural areas. The problem is finding affordable and reliable Internet service for your off-grid location. If you can set up a TV satellite dish, you can have satellite Internet service as well, but the usage fees can be steep.

All said, I really didn't make much money, and I'd have to conclude that there is little money to be made in small towns where you must rely on the locals. The most we made was from selling our ranch when we went back East. Of course, we owned the ranch outright since we paid cash for all materials, buying each board and nail as we could afford it. We didn't go into debt (except for the land, which was carried by the seller for 10 years). This is where freedom begins—staying out of debt.

Bottom line: Be prepared to do whatever it takes, to take jobs that you might not have wanted in another life. Otherwise, be ready to drive into the big city, which I tried as well.

Toward the end of our stay in Arizona, I took a job in Phoenix. The good and bad of it was on par with where I left off when I lost my job back East. It was a job as sales manager for a large building materials manufacturer that was in bankruptcy.

Having firsthand experience with large builders and their concerns while working with a supplier in bankruptcy is a very specialized skill, and I was suddenly in high demand when the recession hit

Phoenix. When the inexperienced managers quit and sought more stable opportunities, I stepped in and cleaned up the messes they left. This didn't mean my position was long term, but it did mean a substantial compensation for taking on an unpleasant task.

The drive from the ranch to Phoenix was too far for a daily commute, but I was able to be home on weekends. The pay was too much to ignore, and we had visions of what we could do on the ranch with the extra money. At the time, real estate in Phoenix was cheap, so we ended up buying a small house in the city. This turned out to be a good financial move for us. Ideally, this would have been where we wanted to be all along. We had the ranch (a paid-off retreat in the boonies) and a small house in a growing area that had a strong job market.

This is how those with money and a job do it, we thought! We enjoyed having a regular (and much larger) income, especially since it allowed us to finish the home projects we had put off until we could afford them. As expected, the job in Phoenix didn't last forever, and when it ended we turned our focus on finishing the repairs on the house in the city. It was to become a two-year house flip, of sorts. After all the work we had done building the ranch, fixing up the house in Phoenix was an easy project.

An interesting note about the little house in Phoenix: it wasn't always a little house. It turned out that our quaint, cozy bungalow was originally a 1920s donkey barn, part of a larger estate that had been subdivided into various parcels. Apparently, there were no standard building controls for donkey barns in the 1920s.

Once we were finished with the remodel, we decided to sell the Phoenix house and regroup at the ranch. It sold quickly, and we were able to return to the high country and get out of the heat.

Just prior to taking the job in Phoenix, my wife and I had become the proud parents of a West Point cadet. By the time the job ended, we were sending two more of our boys (twins) off to college. With this in mind, my wife and I started to take a hard look at what we had learned over the years. We laughed about our youthful expectations and contrasted them to the harsh realities of living off-grid.

At the end of our assessment, we decided that the high desert couldn't keep us in enough tomatoes for our liking. The 20-year drought was still with us, and the 20-mile stretch of dirt road that every gallon of water had to be hauled over was too much for the trucks and our aging bodies. Survival can be accomplished without many things, but not without water. We were ready to find a place that was green and had water on site.

Thus began our three-year search for the *perfect* survival retreat.

SECURITY CONCERNS

Keeping everyone and everything safe and secure takes constant assessment. Our environment changed with each turn we took along the way and always required new thinking. Being able to recognize realistic potential threats is a part of adapting to your environment and is a necessary skill to survive.

TRAVEL SECURITY

To start, we had heavy-duty hasps welded to each of the bus doors and used them with the biggest Master locks we could find. The bus not only served as a vehicle to deliver us to our destination, it was also a mobile vault to stash all our worldly possessions. Keeping the bus safe from intruders was crucial. Today, there are all types of heavy, commercial-quality locks for trucks and vans that look even more secure than what we had. We also installed roll-down curtains on the bus to keep nosey folk from seeing what was inside. Dark tinting would have worked well, too.

When I was a teenager, customized vans were all the rage. I had an old utility Ford Econoline van that I drove to high school. Not having a great-paying job at the time, I couldn't afford a custom window-tinting job like some of my friends had done to their vans and cars, but I could afford some Windex, masking tape, and black spray paint. From inside the van, I cleaned the glass, taped for overspray, and then spray-painted the inside of the windows. After putting up a dark curtain at the front behind the two front seats, there was nothing to see. It was a darker tint than anyone had ever seen before. In fact, I got many compliments about my rear tinted windows and what a great job the tinters had done.

One night my friends and I had been out way too late to go home, so we decided to park the van in the high school lot until morning. That way, we wouldn't miss our morning classes. At some point, the local police showed up and started pounding on the side of the van. We all stayed still and quiet. We could hear the two policemen walk around the van with their flashlights and had to keep from laughing when they held the lights on the rear glass and tried to peer in through the painted windows. We heard one of them comment on how dark the tinting was.

Blacking out windows with paint can be a great option, but check local ordinances to make sure that this is legal in your area. Some states regulate how dark the tinting on vehicle windows can be.

When traveling in a group, especially with the children, we used the mandatory buddy system. No one was allowed to go anywhere alone. This was the rule—no exceptions—and it was never broken.

Although we had several weapons on the bus, they were all locked away out of sight. I did keep my Ruger .357 accessible when we were parked or stopped or camping just in case.

CAMP SECURITY

When we had our camp set up, either in the forest or at a campground, the site was always occupied by me or my wife, or both of us. We did not leave the camp together until we moved onto our own land.

It was possible to lock the tent door with a padlock, but clearly anyone could have gained entrance with just a paper clip through the canvas. The .357 stayed with whoever was at the camp. All said, the forest was safer than the campgrounds. The constant threat of campers watching your every move, along with the occasional drive-by shootings, kept us away from most of the campgrounds. In the forest, we only had to worry about the occasional visitor hiking through . . . and the wild animals, of course.

Once we had our semipermanent site set up on our own land, we could relax a bit about some threats, but we also had to look at new concerns, especially when the visitors were four-footed.

Coyotes were our first concern. They were everywhere, and they make for interesting nights as you lie awake listening to them yip and howl at the moon from just the other side of your canvas wall. We had to bring our dogs in with us at night until we had claimed and staked out our territory. When in a pack, coyotes will try to lure a domestic dog into their midst and then attack it. Our dogs were ready, and most likely were big enough, to hold their own in a fight, but I didn't want to deal with the rabies issues and other injuries that might occur. Soon the pack of coyotes changed their nightly routine to bypass our camp, but they still stopped on the mesa the next forty over from us and sang the blues just long enough to get our dogs barking. Then they would go on their way.

Cattle can also be a security concern for campers, but fortunately in our case they saw us first and stayed clear of camp.

Bears and mountain lions were said to be in the area of Arizona we lived in, but we never saw either while camping out. Soon after we moved back East, a motorist struck one of the biggest mountain lions I've ever seen as it came from an area on our ranch. The only bobcats we saw were also not a threat.

SECURING THE CABIN

At any given time while we were living on our ranch, we had at least two dogs and two cats. All of them did a remarkable—and necessary—job for us.

The dogs acted as our first-alert, early-warning system. They could hear a car or a voice from as far away as a half mile. Once they did, they would run to the driveway barking and letting us know that someone was headed to our ranch. This alone would have been enough for me to be happy with them, but their job didn't end there. They would not stop barking and holding their threatening posture until we called them off. At times, if my wife didn't know who was headed up the driveway, she let the dogs bark and the strangers would leave, not wanting to tangle with the dogs.

The cats had an equally important job keeping us safe from vermin. They kept mice, rats, scorpions, and tarantulas rounded up and away from the cabin. We had one cat that even protected us from the continuous threat of hummingbirds and lizards.

Wearing a sidearm every time you greet strangers is another must. Before we had the fences and gates up, we would have total strangers drive right up to our cabin parking area as if they owned the place. Some were just locals being nosey, while others were looking for cabins to burglarize. Either way, they were unwelcome on our ranch. We soon took to bringing out a black rifle when we met strangers, which worked really well. We never saw the same strangers again, and we had the added benefit of getting a name in town as folks not to mess with.

Once the cabin was occupied, all the guns came out. I had a gun safe, but for the most part we placed the weapons where we had access to them if needed. We had the mandatory 1892 Winchester .357 loaded and hanging over the front door, along with the others loaded and tucked in corners and drawers. We even had a shotgun and pistol hidden away in the outhouse.

We taught all four of our boys to shoot, and they each knew how to work every gun we owned. They knew that, when handled safely, guns are no threat to anyone. They also knew where each gun was located if needed.

In the cabin, we could also lock all the doors and windows when we went to town, and we added the type of heavy-duty security doors popular in big cities with lots of crime.

After seeing the lay of the land and living through a few monsoons, we figured out where the best route for the driveway should be. We added dirt where needed and lined the single lane, 1 1/2-mile-long driveway with logs and rocks. We also included several tight turns and a long stretch clearly visible from the cabin's picture window. This gave would-be trespassers a choice: back out or keep coming. Coming through our gate was the crossing of the Rubicon; after that, there was no turning around. This allowed us to catch those who were casing our home, and we did. Sometimes a pointed conversation was all it took, but other times we had to change the way we did things until the threat passed.

Eventually we learned that the best policy is to have your gate closed and locked at all times. It meant more work for us, but it proved to be the only way to keep people out. When we expected company, we would have one of the boys run out to the gate and leave it open for the guests, but even then we would sometimes have unwanted visitors show up while we were entertaining company. Sometimes you just can't win.

We accidentally discovered an excellent means to slow or catch intruders and trespassers on four-wheelers. When we moved in, an old barbed-wire cross fence ran through our property, a vestige from the original ranch. The fence was 50 or more years old and in rusted but usable condition, as barbed wire goes. I took down the fence and opened up a large field that was approximately 15 acres just to the west of our inner driveway gate. Since the barbed wire was still usable, I wanted to save it for future use. I laid it down in rows across the open field. This was not an issue for us, since we had no livestock on this part of the property.

The next year we had a good monsoon season that brought lots of rain. With the rain came tall grass in our field, obscuring anyone's view of the wire laid out in the field. Then came the four-wheelers. To this day I don't know who they were, just that they were not neighbors. They had most likely come from the city for some family fun tearing up someone else's land—in this case our ranch. We heard them racing up our driveway and started to greet them. They were much faster than we were, and, after seeing that they had ridden nearly up to our cabin, they turned across our field with the tall grass and the barbed wire throughout.

Had the female trespasser's axles not become tangled up in the wire, they would have been successful in their escape across our property. As it turned out, she had to stop to prevent her legs from getting caught up in the wire as it wrapped around the ATV. We helped free the ATV, after explaining that the only exit was back the way they had come. Still, they had made a mess of my wire and the field, and they didn't bother to apologize for trespassing or damaging our land when they left.

It is interesting to note that wagon wheel tracks left by the pioneers of the 1800s are still visible on much of the Old West ranches, as are the four-wheeler's tracks on our property now. Western land is not forgiving of traffic. The better deterrent to trespassers might have been to line our driveway with a barbed wire fence on both sides.

Another security issue you might not have considered is your roof. Like most would-be homesteaders, we had heard about the wonders of the metal roof. They last longer and are more durable, and nothing puts you to sleep faster than the sound of rain on the metal. It had always been our vision to have a cabin with a green metal roof. At first we couldn't afford one, but after a few years we finally got around to capping our 90-pound rolled roofing with green metal. It was everything we had hoped for . . . and some things we hadn't.

For years, our cabin stood alone in the middle of an area of about 1,000 acres with very few other homes or cabins. Once we had put a metal roof on it, we became a target. I mean literally a target. Several military airbases were in the surrounding areas, and once one of the pilots learned of a new target on radar, word spread fast. Our cabin became a popular training mission target for every pilot out there. We would be sitting out on our deck enjoying a cool drink when a low roar would develop from the east. The roar would grow louder and louder until an A-10 Warthog would appear at treetop level and scream over our deck, pulling up as it cleared our ranch. If it wasn't an A-10 it would be an Apache Attack helicopter or another combat aircraft on a training mission with us in its sights.

Another reason topping your retreat with a metal roof is a bad idea is that during a rainstorm you cannot hear anything or anyone approaching. So go with fiberglass-asphalt shingles and hear what's headed your way while also staying off the radar. Taking the time to blend the colors of the shingles to create a sort of camouflage pattern to match your surroundings will also help shield your cabin from satellite photos that many tax assessors are using these days. For a variety of reasons, avoid a metal roof.

FIREARMS
TRAINING

One of the few quality people I met while out West, who is still a great friend of mine, got me started on the right path in my firearms training. When we met, he had just retired from a big-city sheriff's department, where he had served many years as the range master. His job included developing a training routine for deputies, among other things. I was truly fortunate to have him as both a friend and a combat firearms instructor.

His suggested training routine, city street experience, and general shooting philosophy have served many deputies well, and I know that if I were ever involved in a real-life shooting scenario, I would have both the confidence and the ability to do what is necessary to prevail. His style was not unlike what I learned from watching Clint Eastwood on movie nights on the ranch. Keeping a level head while involved in a bad situation will factor into your survival.

When the time came to instruct my sons in combat shooting, I relied heavily on what my friend taught me . . . and Clint Eastwood movies.

"A man's got to know his limitations."
Magnum Force, 1973

As our society continues to spiral downward, it is becoming clear that a simple trip to town can turn into a nasty situation pretty darn quick. Banks, convenience stores, restaurants, and many other commonly visited city places have seen near riots like our country has rarely seen before. Often these dangerous situations are sparked by issues once thought to be of little concern. Our society is on the brink, a powder keg, fused and at the ready. Some of us have learned that we don't even have to leave our homes to be attacked. More and more, people who once thought conditions couldn't get that bad are running out and purchasing handguns because they have indeed gotten that bad.

Dangerous situations are often out of our control, and we don't know when they may come up or what our level of involvement may be. As individuals, we can enter these situations either knowing our limitations or having little or no idea of what our abilities really are or how we will perform. Yet, this is the one area that we actually can have some control over.

Knowing your limitations is the best gauge of knowing when you're in real trouble, which is why we all should strive to know our limitations. To know what our limitations are, however, we must first measure our ability.

Clearly, the first step in getting to know our shooting abilities can be accomplished with continued practice. As the old saying goes, "Practice makes perfect," or at least it can make us better at what we are practicing. As we get better with practice, we gain a realistic confidence in our abilities. As we gain a realistic confidence in our abilities, we come to understand what we can do in real terms and then can know our limitations. This can be used to keep us out of trouble (best case) or get us out of trouble (worst case), as well as keeping others safe.

KNOW YOUR WEAPON

"Being as this is a .44 Magnum, the most powerful handgun in the world, and would blow your head clean off . . ."
Dirty Harry, **1971**

There are as many opinions about what is the best handgun to carry as there are people carrying handguns. I have just one rule to suggest: go with the best gun you can afford that sits correctly and comfortably in your hand. When you draw the gun from its holster or pick it up and sight a target, does the gun naturally sit in your hand in a position where the sights line up correctly without repositioning it? If so, this would be a compatible handgun for you.

Hogue produces grips that can improve nearly any handgun and make your grip better than many stock grips. If you find a gun that has features you like but doesn't feel right in your hand, try it out with alternative grips before giving up on it. Grips are very easy to replace. Once you have determined which guns with which grips meet this standard, then go with the best quality you can afford.

Whichever handgun you choose to carry, know your weapon. Be entirely familiar with it: how it functions, how many rounds it holds, what safety devices (if any) it has. As you begin your target practicing, be sure to include the review and use of the safety and other gun functions.

PRACTICE MAKES PERFECT

Proper practice requires more than grabbing a 50-round box of ammo and your sidearm and heading to the range for some shooting. Yes, there is much to be said for consistently hitting your target, but once you have reached that level of proficiency, adding a few slight modifications to your range practice will get you closer to knowing your true abilities, which are what will see you through real-life threats.

Consider what conditions might exist that would force you to use your weapon for defense. Where might you be—at the bank, convenience store, or home? Do you carry concealed? What type of holster do you use? And be sure to add your holster to your practice routine. Whether you carry concealed or open, start your practice sequence with a casual stance and then draw from your preferred holster position and place your shots. Galco Gunleather makes a large variety of both concealed and unconcealed holsters for almost every handgun made. If you use several types of holsters, practice with them all.

> **"I know what you're thinking. 'Did he fire six shots
> or only five?' Well, to tell you the truth, in all this
> excitement, I kind of lost track myself."**
> *Dirty Harry,* 1971

This would also be a good time to train yourself in counting rounds. Harry Callahan knew exactly how many rounds he had fired. You should, too. Knowing how many rounds of ammo you have left may prove to be important if you ever have to defend yourself against a home invader and his friends in your hallway.

SO, JUST HOW FAST ARE YOU?

Once you have put in enough range time to be reasonably consistent in all of the above, you will be ready for the next level in your quest for Callahan-like confidence: measuring your speed. Midway USA offers electronic devices known as shot timers, such as the Competition Electronics Pocket Pro.

With such a timer, you can measure the time (in hundredths of a second) from the sound of a beep emitted by the timer to the sound of your gun's report. Other models can be programmed to measure the second report or even more depending on what your sequence requires. Continued practice at this level will tell the real story about your abilities and limitations. My original practice sequence was based on an open-carry holster and was as follows:

1. I start in a relaxed stance (but alert condition), with my hands in front and together.
2. The shot timer beep sounds, alerting me to draw and fire.
3. My right hand (I am right-handed) drops to the holster, my thumb breaks the retaining snap, and my hand draws the weapon from the holster and raises sights to eye level.
4. I acquire the target (10-inch steel plate at head level, 20 feet away).
5. I fire two shots on target.

Note: Always pay close attention when setting up steel targets to be certain they are angled *down* to the ground so that you don't put yourself in danger from ricochets thrown back at you.

My best measured time in completing the sequence was 1.52 seconds, and my running average was about 1.60 seconds. By many standards this is considered slow, like molasses in wintertime (OK, I have watched *The Outlaw Josie Wales* a few times, too), but consider all that is done in that 1.6 seconds.

Later, I added two more targets to my sequence to simulate three threats. I later added practice with a concealed holster (Galco Jackass rig).

At all stages of your sequence practice, be aware that time is everything. Having picked a gun that sits and feels right in your hand may have saved you 1/10 of a second. Having the right holster can save you even more time. Practicing your draw can also shave fractions of seconds from your overall time. Of course, consistency in hitting the target is an absolute must for the drill.

Once you have worked your sequence, you can then start breaking it down to learn where you can save more time. Having a partner watch you run through your drill and suggest where you spend too much time can also be a great help. In the end, only you can decide how fast you need to be in order to gain the confidence needed for any likely threats you may face. Practice to that level or until you are as fast as you will be.

THE PHILOSOPHY BEHIND THE KNOWLEDGE

"Nothing wrong with shooting, as long as the right people get shot!"
Magnum Force, 1973

I know we can all agree that we never want to shoot the wrong people. The best defensive weapon we carry everywhere everyday is our mind. Staying alert and processing what we see and hear, while outwardly remaining Callahan-like calm and cool, is our best defense. Having a common situation turn south into a life-threatening event would have us then waiting for the beep to go off in our heads, but knowing your limitations and abilities allows you more time to react. Let's say, for example, your best time from a concealed holster to two placed shots in a 10-inch circle is two seconds. Knowing that you have the ability to end a threat in two seconds affords you the extra time needed to evaluate the situation more clearly.

You are now operating from a position of power. You have done more than memorize cool lines from the *Dirty Harry* movies; you actually know your limitations.

Evaluate the threat. Does he look like the kind of guy who spends a lot of time at the range practicing, or does he just watch the *Dirty Harry* reruns? Is his gun clean and cared for, or is it covered in grease, dust, and lint? Is it an old piece or new? Is he continuously repositioning the gun in his hand as he turns and looks around while he is evaluating his situation? What is his reaction time to changing events at the scene? Does he know his limitations? Is he nervous? Is he shaking? Are you?

Knowing that you can end a life-threatening situation in two seconds can give you the extra time needed to determine whether the situation is beyond your limitations. It will also give you the confidence that your decision is the correct one.

When your assailant turns his gun on you, he has clearly crossed the threshold of threatening your life. How long will you allow that threat against you to last before you decide to end it? Maybe you can talk him down without having to draw your weapon, and he'll leave without anyone getting shot. Maybe things will turn for the worst, and you'll be forced to take action. But it will be *your* moment. *You* will decide.

TOOLS OF
THE TRADE

The following is about the typical tools that spring to mind when you hear the term *tools*: hammers, rakes, utility knives, and so forth. But before discussing these more conventional tools, I want to mention two other "tools" that I think belong in every successful survivalist's toolbox: books and weapons.

BOOKS

There is one thing we are not short on in the survivalist community: information. Preppers may keep information about what they *have* to themselves but are typically willing to share whey they *know* with others. After all, the more people we can get to prepare, the fewer refugees there will be knocking at our door.

In my mind, having the right information available is just as important as having food or shelter. Although much can be learned from visiting such Internet sites as TheSurvivalistBlog.net, Survival-Blog.net, or Americanpreppersnetwork.net, I am a true believer in owning good, old-fashioned printed books. If there were ever to be an EMP or solar flare event that knocked out the power grid and fried delicate circuitry, you'd learn quickly that a hard drive was *not* the best place to store all your survival info after all.

Our library, which we use on a regular basis, includes most of what Paladin Press offers, along with books on subjects such as chickens, goats, rabbits, general livestock, fishing, hunting, trapping, canoeing, mountain climbing, search and rescue, and other living-off-the-land-related subjects. Knowing how to set and splint a broken leg or drain an abscess is vital information if a doctor is not in your mutual aid group—or even if you have one in your group. Who knows whether trained personnel will be available when and where you need them? So first aid books are well represented in our library.

Everyone in our family is a voracious reader, so, of course, we have our literature collection, including classics and modern works from such masters as Stephen King and Gary Larson. Since we homeschooled our boys, we also have a number of reference and instructional books related to that, which still come in handy more often than you'd think.

WEAPONS

Defensive weapons such as guns and knives are definitely at the top of the list of required tools. Everyone in your group should have at least one of each. Ideally, you will also be able to outfit a straggler who joins the group as well. You can never have too many guns or knives at the retreat. What aren't used can eventually be traded for what is needed.

CONVENTIONAL TOOLS

In addition to their value as work implements, all tools make desirable bartering stock. My truck stops at every yard or estate sale it passes. Fishing poles and tools are at the top of my to-buy list. It is unfortunate, but many of the tools made today just don't last. I still have the first set of wrenches I bought when I got my first car, and I keep my grandfather's tools in the same box he used to carry to work every day. His tools are in better condition than mine. Of course, his were made in the United States at a time when no one would have considered buying tools from anywhere else, while mine were made in China.

Most garden tools also come from China these days, but you can still find some older, "made in the USA" tools in good condition at farm and yard sales across the country. Buy all you can get a good deal on. Today's inferior tools break and will have to be replaced. Having 10 good shovels in the shed just means you'll get that hole dug more efficiently *and* you'll have much-in-demand barter shovels down the road.

The types of tools I consistently look for and buy are:

- Rakes of all types, especially metal
- Hoes
- Posthole diggers
- Splitting mauls and axes
- Grain and meat grinders
- Cast-iron pots, pans, and spiders (three-legged skillets)
- Water tanks and barrels
- Seamless stainless steel pots (for milking)
- Drawknives
- Crosscut saws
- Log bars (dogs and peelers)
- Digging irons
- Brace and bit drill sets and hand drills
- Files, all types
- Hand planers
- Handsaws
- Blacksmithing tools and furnaces
- Farrier tools
- Complete wrench sets
- Fencing tools (pullers and dikes)
- Loppers and machetes
- Quality knives
- Woodman's Pal machetes

Owning gas-powered tools is always an option, but remember

that they'll be useful only as long as the gas supply continues to flow. Remember, too, that my boys and I built our Arizona cabin without the use of power tools. It can be done.

It can be overwhelming when you consider what you will be doing in a worst-case scenario and what tools you'll need to help complete the tasks at hand. Many people just start buying stuff (as, alas, we did) before really considering what the basic tools should consist of.

Start by outfitting each of your family members with the best-quality tools you can afford. The basics listed below are what you would carry in your bug-out bag and are the tools you would never be without.

- Sidearm and ammunition
- Fixed-blade knife, such as the Becker BK2
- Multitool, such as the Gerber Leatherman
- Woodman's Pal or traditional machete
- Tritium compass
- Boots, socks, coat, hat, gloves, and raingear
- Katadyn Pocket water filter
- Aurora Fire Starter 440C with Magnesium

Once these basics have been covered, you can add tools to complement your situation.

MUTUAL AID GROUPS
AND LIKE-MINDED FRIENDS

Earlier in the book I talked about our three older boys participating in the local high school's sports programs, despite their being homeschooled. The advice I gave my boys before we let them loose on the world was simply, "Keep your mouth shut as long as you can."

It didn't take long before we realized which of them took heed of the advice. Our oldest son remained quiet the longest about his interests and likes, and soon became a man of mystery and intrigue at school. He sat back and listened to everyone and was then able to choose whom he wanted to befriend based on his choice rather than being chosen by others.

The same advice applies to adults. Maintaining your privacy goes hand-in-hand with being a survivalist. When moving into a new community, it has always been my goal to remain as invisible and private as possible until I was able to sort out who was who. When you're new to an area, it is easy to become the target of thieves and burglars who have been watching your vacant house long before you arrived. New doors, locks, fences, and gates have always been the first order of business for me when I move to a new place.

Having extra cars in the driveway, leaving random lights on in the house when possible, keeping the gate locked, and posting your land all work to keep the wrong element off your property.

The "good old days" of communities inhabited by like-minded people, often close friends and extended family members, are just about gone. Looking out for each other was second nature in most neighborhoods back then. Today, we either don't get to know our neighbors at all or we fear them. When we lived in close-knit communities, things got done at the local level and didn't require the input of various government agencies, from the local yokels clear on up to the feds. Now nothing gets done since there is no way to please all the strangers who make up our diverse communities. In today's society, we are told that diversity is desirable and that we must be tolerant of all types of people and ideas.

Don't get me wrong: diversity in a survival group is good. Including people in your group who have firsthand knowledge of survival-related skills—such as firearms; emergency medicine; hunting, fishing, and trapping; gardening; raising livestock; construction—dramatically increases your chances of weathering whatever storm blows your way. But all members of the group must agree on common goals. To survive the coming societal collapse, we must, at some level, reestablish a community of like-minded people who will *not* tolerate an attack on our freedoms. What was once known as an average American community is now being called a "mutual aid group."

By far the most advantageous situation to be in is to have at least one other survivalist group with whom your group has a mutual aid agreement. This is true for many reasons. First, there is safety in numbers. In a worst-case scenario, having additional armed allies covering your rear is always a good thing. In Arizona, we had a like-minded neighbor between the main road and us, so we made a mutual agreement to watch each other's back. Plus, we each knew that we could retreat to the other's place if we needed to.

Under less serious circumstances, being part of a collection of two or more groups has many advantages. It creates an opportunity to get accurate information about what is happening in the surrounding areas through a free exchange of information and news. It allows the trading of goods and services as needed by each group in order to get important surplus supplies to those who need it most. Further, there is a social benefit to having mutual aid groups, as most of us are social beings and need fellowship with like-minded people.

One of the most difficult things for a prepper to prepare for is the moment you're faced with turning away someone from your door. Who will you have to turn away? For most of us, it will be your neighbor or his wife, along with their little girl with her sad, hungry face . . . the same folks who flew to Miami three weeks ago for an expensive, last-minute hookup with some old college chums. It was just another vacation they couldn't afford but took anyway. After all, you only live once. Your son fed their dog and cat, just like he always does when they're away. Your family is known for always being available for such tasks since you never take vacations.

It's true. You haven't gone on vacation for many years. Your disposable funds have been going into silver and gold bullion, storable grains, dried beans, canned foods, and guns and ammo. That's why you're content behind your locked doors. You saw the approaching storm and prepared for it. Several times you tried to warn your neighbors about the pending collapse, but they ignored you.

It would be wonderful if everyone prepared for emergencies and could bring something to the table to share with the group. But that's not going to happen. And if you are unprepared when the SHTF, it will be *you* who is either a refugee or an unwanted liability. Few prepared families will be seeking another mouth to feed. If that's the case, you'd better have a comfortable pair of walking shoes, because you'll be doing a lot of walking.

The alternative is to take the time now to seek out websites and blogs that offer free advice to preppers. Read all you can about the conditions that could follow various types of collapses and start gathering the supplies needed to see you and your family through the coming hard times. Make your home site defensible or find a property you can retreat to easily if you must evacuate. Even if you aren't fully prepared to survive on your own, you will have supplies, knowledge, and skills to share when you approach like-minded neighbors or groups for assistance.

For people who are setting up a retreat in a new community, there is a strong case to be made for maintaining a low profile and not making any friends until you can determine who can be trusted. This can take a long time, even years, to figure out, but there are ways to speed up the process.

Small communities are, for the most part, closed. They are inhabited by long-time residents who have known each other for many years. The families that have been there for generations will always consider you an outsider. You have to work around this obstacle as best you can.

Once you've secured your retreat, go to the local co-op and introduce yourself. Project the image of yourself you want them to see. Divulge nothing that you don't want every single person in the community to know. Talk to the staff about such activities as gardening, beekeeping, or livestock. Ask if they are familiar with your new property and tell them how much you are enjoying living there. Maybe you will learn something about its history that the seller didn't disclose. Ask about the local fishing holes and festivals, and make note of worthwhile community information revealed, especially any criminal incidents or trouble that might have occurred. Someone will tell you most of what you need to know about your new community.

A visit to the local police or sheriff's department might also be a good idea. Introduce yourself and ask about the area, especially any problems or concerns you should know about. Join the local volunteer fire department. Go to all the meetings and take all the free training offered to members, especially EMT, paramedic, technical rescue, and search and rescue training. Volunteer at the sheriff's department or with the sheriff's auxiliary. Your participation in these activities will not only allow you to contribute to your new community and remain up to date with issues that affect you, it will also make you aware of other survivalists in the community.

Be cautious when approaching any like-minded person about forming a group. You need to establish trust and understanding before disclosing what your resources are and where they are stored. Also be wary of the person who is well armed but doesn't have an adequate store of food, water, and other supplies. I met one such self-proclaimed survivalist out West who would infiltrate small groups of preppers to map out where to raid if the SHTF. Fortunately, he was also a bit of a braggart, and people wised up to his plan before he could steal anyone's provisions. Word spread quickly about him, and now every survivalist in the area is ready to deal with him should he show up uninvited.

For us, it is family first where group membership is concerned. We do have several groups of friends who are all survivalists and might be expected to knock on our door in a crisis. But we know that they have all prepared themselves for likely emergencies, and that our place is plan B for them. And we know that we can go to their places if we need to as well. But family is a different story. Even if relatives don't prepare in advance, expect them and have extra gear and food for them when they arrive. Just let them know that the rule of the house is, "You work, you eat."

As preppers, we feel responsible for everyone we claim as ours. I can't imagine anyone turning away Mamaw or Aunt Betty, so I have planned ahead and set aside extra beans and rice to cover anyone who shows up at the last minute.

I also have enough to give the neighbors and their small daughter a meal or two to see them down the road. Unfortunately, I cannot feed everyone.

CONCLUSIONS, RECOMMENDATIONS, AND FINAL THOUGHTS

By the end of our time in Arizona, we had learned quite a bit about living off the grid and being self-sufficient. All the lessons were important, of course, but perhaps the biggest lesson we learned was that *water is everything.*

Of the 15 years we lived out West, all were spent dealing with drought. Arizona is in a continuous state of drought, as is most of Southern California, Nevada, New Mexico, and most of the rest of the western United States. There is no end in sight for this drought. Our boys were raised thinking that rivers were dusty, low-lying ribbons of dirt that ran through the desert. Our youngest son couldn't understand how fish lived in the dirt. It took my wife seven years to actually have a worthwhile tomato harvest.

What is called a drought in the East is nothing compared to those in the West. A drought in the eastern United States starts with having some water, while the western drought starts with having none. Further, the water supplies in the West are constantly being challenged in the courts. The states know there is not enough water to supply the uncontrolled growth and fight over every drop. The Hoover Dam was even raised to hold additional water, as if the completion of the project would bring the rains.

The issue comes down to the fact that there are too many people in the Southwest for the supply of water that exists. I fail to see how a court is going to order more water. As it was, we did not even have the rights to the rainwater that fell on our ranch! This was just as well, since if the six of us had to survive off the rainwater that fell on our ranch, we surely would have perished.

There are few places on Earth as unique and beautiful as the American Southwest, but we had seen enough. We wanted green. We wanted tomatoes and corn. We wanted the right to collect any rainwater that fell on our own property, and we wanted a real lake, pond, river, or stream that had fish in it. We wanted to make preserves out of a fruit that didn't have needles sticking out of it.

Make no mistake. All the heirloom seeds, fine animals, and stored provisions will amount to nothing without enough water to plant, hydrate, and cook with. There are some areas of the West that do have local water supplies, but most of the West relies on water from somewhere else. It is only the rule of law that allows those areas to continue getting their water. When the rule of law goes away, so will the water supply to those areas.

Every lesson my family and I learned during the time we spent out West we applied to our new venture: going back East. The ranch sold quickly. We were left with just our shop to use as a storage facility, and we bought a travel trailer to use as we started looking for a better retreat location. The next two years were spent traveling, only to find ourselves a day too late in making an offer. When we finally were able to find a suitable lot that hadn't been sold already, we had to move quickly.

At the time, we were staying at a friend's house in the East and were snowbound by a series of storms that had bombarded the area. I found the lot on the Internet and contacted the agent. She was local to the area where the lot was but said that the roads were impassable at that time due to the snow. We waited three days and then, on the first day the sun reemerged, we met her at the lot. As it turned out, there were several agents with prospective buyers just as eager for the land. We happened to be the first on-site and actually met two groups of agents as we were leaving.

We had a few things going for us. The agents didn't know where the true lot lines were located (but we did), and we had cash from the

"Water, water, everywhere!" The river on our eastern property.

sale of our ranch. I had to pull out our final ace by making a full-price offer to ensure that we got the lot. We did, and the property turned out to be far better than just suitable.

The new retreat property is approximately 100 acres and has water. Not only is it in a region that gets about 50 inches of rain a year, but the property has a small river running through it. The river has at least eight varieties of fish that we have caught so far and draws all kinds of wildlife. Plus, the land is abundant with the natural fruits and vegetation of the area.

The mountain has wild blueberries, blackberries, and apples. As far as wildlife goes, we have seen as many as 30 turkeys at one time on the land, as well as deer, grouse, opossum, raccoon, and bear. It was truly a wonderful find, and we know we are blessed to own it.

The downside is that we bought a piece of land that is the secret fishing and hunting spot for the inhabitants of five surrounding counties. We have had trespassers like we'd never have imagined. They are everywhere. They run their dogs across our land at night and bring their kids fishing on our land during the day. They bring their cousins on our land when deer season opens, and they bring their wives four-wheeling down our driveway on Saturday mornings before breakfast. We have had our lives threatened by intruders, sometimes at gunpoint, when we suggested that they were trespassing on private land.

It has only been through the extensive use of barbed wire, posted no trespassing signs, and legal prosecution that we have slowed the tide of those who say they have a blood right to trespass on our land since their great-granddaddy trespassed there a hundred years ago. No kidding—we actually had a few of them suggest just that! Be prepared for the same if you find the perfect piece of ground in rural America. And make sure that you have thoroughly researched the plot you are interested in for any existing easements or rights-of-way grants, as well as the land-use laws in the state and county where the land is located. You don't want to be surprised by any adverse or hostile possession action by parties who have been using the land before you acquired it.

When you do find your ground, build a cabin (with a shingled roof). Trailers are good protection from bears while you build, but they show up on instrumentation (e.g., FLIR) easily and have too many other issues to be of any real use other than temporary housing. Tents are the next best choice for a survival retreat; they don't show up on radar, but they aren't for everyone. My wife lasted a year and a half in ours, but I may never get her back in one again.

Even if you are paying on your land, don't finance your cabin. Pay as you go. Get out of all debt as soon as you can. If you are doing this while working at a good job, keep your retreat in the

We used pine beams in the construction of our eastern cabin, as we had in Arizona. Through the service of WildBlue and our solar power, we were able to get online from a very remote, off-grid location.

paid-off column of your finances. Being debt-free is freedom in and of itself.

Start with primitive living and move up in the world as you can afford to. Make your cabin livable before spending money on the

Busted! One of the mistakes we made while building our eastern cabin was putting a metal roof on it. Realizing our mistake, we replaced it with an asphalt-shingled roof as soon as we could.

expensive upgrades. You just may find that you prefer oil lamps to electric lights. Frame, insulate, and wire your cabin to the building code for legal reasons as well as your own safety. Go with a fiberglass-shingled roof so that it is less visible from the air and you can hear approaching threats during a heavy rain.

Always carry your sidearm, no matter where you go or what you do. There can be threats around every corner.

No matter how cool it might look, don't ever use a kerosene-fueled cookstove. These were very popular during the Great Depression, and they are still made today. They use a quart jar of oil, turned upside down to feed a simple, flat-wick design that produces

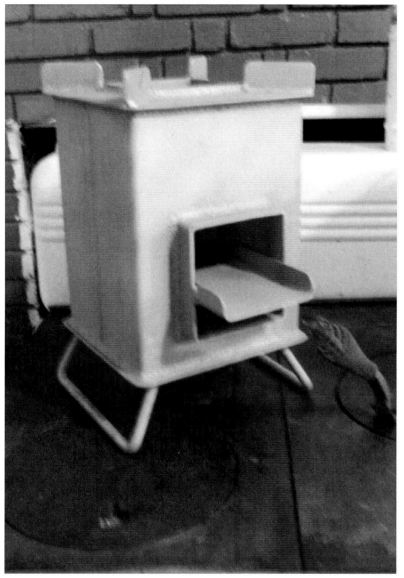

Our Grover Rocket Stove goes everywhere with us.

a lot of soot. It is my supposition that it was actually the depressing looks of people who used these stoves that led to the naming of this era, Great Depression!

I found that the Grover Rocket Stove is not only the best designed but also the best constructed; it is pretty near bulletproof. Mine has been bouncing around in the back of my truck and is as good as new. It is a much better design than a kerosene stove, and it uses free fuel (i.e., firewood or any dry plant material). It is made for cooking outdoors, but if you have a masonry fireplace you could use it to cook in the hearth.

For winter indoor cooking, get a drop-in countertop gas range. Most will readily convert to propane and run for months on one tank of propane (100-pound bottle). As for a night-light, light heat, and the quick heating of soup or coffee, it's the Dietz 2500 Jupiter lantern, hands-down.

FINAL THOUGHTS

Our nation is coming apart at the seams. Whether by inevitable natural phenomenon or by man's evil conspiracy, individually and collectively as a nation we are facing a future that may never be recorded in the history books of tomorrow. Much of the Dark Ages and what went on during that period in history has been lost, as I suspect much of what is to come will be as well.

The very real prospects of super storms, volcanoes, earthquakes, tyranny, war, famine, disease, monetary collapse, and social breakdown are discussed casually on the morning news as we eat our Krispy Kremes and drink our coffee and pay little attention to the dire predictions. Therefore, few realize what is coming.

No one will be as prepared as they should, and some will be prepared far better than others. Some will not have given the signs of what is on its way a second look and will have nothing set aside to see them even through the devastation.

If you have done nothing to prepare, if you think you'll ride this out at home, if you have no plan, please know this much: eventually you may have to leave your home, either as a volunteer or lying down in a coffin. For some, the finale will be in the defense of their home and all they have worked for in preparation for these times. Others will either surrender to a superior and more deadly force or choose to leave one day in order to live the next day. If you choose to leave, you'll either be a refugee, subject to the flow of the masses of people who did not prepare and are seeking food and shelter, or you will be able to avoid the mob and keep to yourself or your group until things settle down.

Having a bug-out bag could make the difference between being a refugee and being a free individual, between being bound to the refugee camp or being able to leave. The simplest bag is described on page 136, but a better-equipped bag for a societal SHTF scenario should have, at the very least, these items:

- Aurora fire starter/matches/Bic lighters
- Tinder
- Good survival knife and multitool
- Tritium compass
- Area map
- Handgun and ammo
- High-calorie energy bars and electrolyte replacements
- Small first aid kit
- Personal medications and vitamins
- Small Cree LED flashlight
- Paracord and poncho
- Water bladder, iodine pills, and canteen
- Space blanket
- Needle, thread, dental floss
- Small fishing kit

Keep everything secure in your bag with lanyards and added closures. Your life may depend on any one of these items, which will become scarce faster than you can imagine. Wear all the clothes you want to keep and stock energy food in whatever space is left in your bag. If you are to travel with others, you can start adding more shelter items. Those who travel alone won't be sleeping much.

Above all, if you have ever thought about taking the path my family took, if you ever have thought about becoming more self-sufficient, or if you just want to move forward with your survival plans, do it now. What are you waiting for? Life is short, and time to prepare is growing even shorter. I wish you well in your adventure.

RESOURCES

ALTE
Solar panels and control units
http://www.altestore.com/store

BERKEY WATER FILTERS
Stainless steel countertop water filters
http://www.berkeyfilters.com

CAMMENGA COMPASS
Tritium compass
http://www.cammenga.com

COLEMAN'S MILITARY SURPLUS
Good military surplus, camping, and survival gear
http://www.colemans.com

FRESH WATER SYSTEMS
Cabin water system filters by Rusco and others
http://www.freshwatersystems.com

GROVER ROCKET STOVES
The best heavy-duty stove on the market
http://www.stockstorage.com

GSI OUTDOORS
Stainless steel coffee percolator
http://www.gsioutdoors.com

KATADYN WATER FILTERS
The best portable filter
http://www.katadyn.com

MAXPEDITION
Hard-use bags and packs
http://www.maxpedition.com

MOUNTAIN GEAR SURPLUS SALES
GP Med tents
http://armytents.com

NUUN ELECTROLYTE REPLACEMENT TABS
Electrolyte replacement and hydration
http://www.nuun.com

PALADIN PRESS
Action Library for survival, self-defense, and combat shooting books
and videos
http://www.paladin-press.com

SOLO SCIENTIFIC
Aurora Fire Starter, which throws 5,000°F sparks!
http://soloscientific.com

SPEEDHOOK.COM
Survival fishing and trapping gear
http://www.speedhook.com/servlet/StoreFront

W.T. KIRKMAN OIL & ELECTRIC LAMPS AND LANTERNS
Dietz oil lanterns
http://lanternnet.com

WILDERNESS SOLUTIONS
Alternative fire starter
http://www.wildersol.com

WOODMAN'S PAL
Land-clearing and survival machetes
http://www.woodmanspal.com

ABOUT THE AUTHOR

The only thing F.J. Bohan enjoys more than living in the mountains is a good conversation over a great cup of coffee. He is a musician, gun enthusiast, amateur prospector, and dog and cat lover. When not helping his wife with their small orchard, vineyard, and berry farm, he can be found fishing or canoeing on their private mountain stream. He is currently hoping to see more bears and learn to play the banjo while promoting his books. With more than 25 years of practical experience in surviving under adverse conditions, he is happy to share what he has learned.

He can be reached with questions, comments, or stories at fjbohan.com.